THE INDIVIDUATION OF GOD

THE INDIVIDUATION OF GOD

Integrating Science and Religion

PETER B. TODD

CHIRON PUBLICATIONS

WILMETTE, ILLINOIS

Book and cover design by Marianne Jankowski.
Printed in the United States of America.

Library of Congress Cataloging-in-Publication Data

Todd, Peter B.
The individuation of God : integrating science and religion / Peter B. Todd.
    p. cm.
Includes bibliographical references (p.   ) and index.
1. Religion and science. I. Title.
BL240.3.T63 2012
201'.65--dc23

                                                    2012024335

CONTENTS

FOREWORD

For who knows what is good for
a man in life, during the few and
meaningless days he passes through like
a shadow? Who can tell him what will
happen under the sun after he is gone?
(Ecclesiastes 6:12, NIV)

In this book, Peter Todd has tackled the hardest questions there are—how we understand and make meaningful our human consciousness, how we apprehend and transcend the concepts of time and space, the temporal and eternal, and the contrived dichotomies of science and religion, the secular and the sacred, the material and the ethereal—in his search for a theology of the third millennium, Todd rejects the arguments both for and against Western religion, with its anthropomorphic god, its spatial concepts of heaven and hell, and its temporal concept of life after death. Rather, like Carl Jung, he argues for a collective unconscious that reaches back into prehistory but remains alive in all of us, thereby creating a transcendent state of interconnectedness and an endless spatiality and temporality. Nietzsche and Freud were both sympathetic to this view. Nietzsche viewed dreams as "some primeval relic of humanity [that] is at work which we can now scarcely reach any longer by a direct path" (Freud 1900, p. 549). Freud believed that "each individual somehow recapitulates in an abbreviated form the entire development of the human race...[yet] these phylogenetic inheritances are freshly acquired in the development of the individual" (Freud 1916, p. 199). The form of this development, however, belongs to ontogeny, the individual's prehistory (infancy). Todd recognizes this problem for connectedness. Without individual psyches there would be no theory. James Joyce also struggled with this question: "What can each man know but what passes through his mind?" A great deal has passed through the mind of Peter Todd in this challenging and timely work. There is an inherent optimism in collectivism and timelessness. At the end of the book, we are left to ponder Jung's question as to whether we are connected to the infinite or not.

Dianna T. Kenny, Ph.D.
Professor of Psychology
The University of Sydney

PREFACE

One common delusion about God is that theological propositions about concepts and experiences of the numinous have become meaningless and imponderable due to lessons in how to make one's ideas clear from such logical positivists as Bertrand Russell and his pupil Ludwig Wittgenstein and members of the once elite Vienna Circle of philosophers. Within this philosophical framework, the so-called "God hypothesis" cannot be shown to be either true or false empirically and therefore is not to be spoken of as a meaningful scientific question. Rather it is to be passed over in silence. However, skeptics such as biologist Richard Dawkins, author of *The God Delusion* (2006), far from considering God to be dead as a result of developments in science and philosophy, regard the existence of religion as "the root of all evil," while in literature, Christopher Hitchens perceives religious belief systems to be positively toxic in his book *God Is Not Great: How Religion Poisons Everything* (2007).

In reality, however, the project of deicide is far from complete, perhaps because the idea of the numinous is an integral aspect of humankind's quest for a sense of transpersonal meaning and self-transcendence. From a depth psychological perspective and in the Jungian tradition, for instance, the unconscious God archetype and numinous symbols of the Self are psychic facts that require explanation rather than being simply denied or dismissed by a rationalist philosophy in which reason is dissolved by skeptical zealotry and hostility.

One of the aims of this book is to address the need for a theology that may be less vulnerable to intemperate or militant criticism and also illuminated by scientific perspectives on fundamental issues pertinent to both science and theology, for instance, the psychophysical or mind/matter problem and the understanding of the so-called "arrow of time" and its relationship to timelessness in both post-quantum physics and depth psychology. These two fields have been thought to stand in a relationship of complementarity by such eminent physicists as Wolfgang Pauli and David Bohm, to whom I shall refer at length, especially in chapters 3 and 4.

Richard Dawkins and his skeptical colleagues do not seem to me to have grasped how central such questions still are to Erwin Schrödinger's questions about life, mind, and matter and to a contemporary theology (1992). Archbishop of Canterbury Rowan Williams refers to this contemporary theology as conceiving God as "an eternal and unconditioned reality," incarnational in nature and compatible with evolution insofar as it envisions humanity as completing the becoming of God ("Williams Questions Dawkins' Critical Thinking," 2007, n.p.). The reductionist materialist position that mind and consciousness are simply epiphenomenal and causally inefficacious by-products of brain process is seriously challenged in light of recent developments in neuroscience as well as in quantum physics and depth psychology. Yet such a reductionist position, together with the strangulation of mind by the spatiotemporal hold of classical physics, is indispensable to arguments advanced by the skeptics and atheists considered in detail here.

Apropos the numinous, I consider the implications for theology of Bohm's concept of the implicate order, with active information providing a bridge between the mental and the physical, and of the formulation by both Jung and Pauli of the unconscious archetypes as cosmic ordering and regulating principles whose influence is observable in both the external (phenomenal) and internal worlds. Both notions imply the significance of influences independent of space and time, something of an embarrassment for rationalist materialists. I suggest that the grasp of mind and depth psychology by some of the more vociferous skeptics is quite rudimentary so that their treatment of consciousness is flawed, while the so-called meme hypothesis as an explanation of cultural evolution is an empirically vacuous idea.

In chapters 1 and 2, I canvass the case against God put forward by such skeptics as Dawkins and Hitchens while providing a critique of religious fundamentalism and its final destination. I revisit the traditional neo-Darwinian paradigm of evolution and consider such Kuhnian anomalies as directed and adaptive mutation as well as difficulties within the paradigm in explaining the origins of life as well as the emergence of mind (Wallace's problem with Darwin) and the reflective consciousness necessary for humankind's highest cultural achievements in both science and culture, including religion. Perspectives on the psychophysical problem are elaborated in light of developments in such diverse disciplines as quantum physics and information theory, neuroscience, consciousness studies, and depth psychology.

Chapters 3 and 4 further explore the nuances of the mind/brain relationship, considering particularly the contributions of Bohm and Pauli to the idea of the complementarity of mind and matter. I will also look at the contributions of depth psychologists C. G. Jung, Michael Fordham, and others to the understanding of unconscious symbols and manifestations of the numinous, including the God archetype and its connection to the Self in its timeless aspects. Chapter 4 takes up the theme of a scientifically informed theology enriched by depth psychological understanding of archetypal symbols of the numinous and of mystical experience, including the cosmic religious feelings reported by scientists. Also in chapter 4, I will revisit the psychoanalytic concept of illusion as the foundation of culture and religion explored by such notable analysts as Donald Winnicott and Jesuit William Meissner.

Chapter 5 begins by discussing the role of myth and symbol in religious transformation as well as in transformation facilitated by analytically oriented psychotherapies while exposing religious fundamentalism in its various guises as the real delusion about God. Chapter 5 then presents an elaborate treatment of the "religion" of metaphysical materialism, particularly those aspects masquerading as political and economic ideologies and implying the virtual apotheosis of charismatic cult leaders such as Hitler, Stalin, and Mao. The religion of metaphysical materialism, I suggest, menaces the earth with the threat of global warming because the sense of the numinous and the collective, global experience of the sacredness of the planet have been replaced by an idolatry of money, power, and possession of finite resources.

Chapter 6 integrates the themes of the previous chapters in a mythopoeic description of what a third millennium theology might look like. It attempts to resolve the question raised by Schrödinger of whether time will eventually destroy its own creator and presents a solution to the psychophysical problem that would permit theology to evolve rather than becoming an anachronism or a fossil in the history of ideas. Crucial to this development is the notion of a consciousness that is not simply epiphenomenal. The traditional doctrine of the incarnation is extended to include the unorthodox idea of a future evolution of God through humankind: humanity completing God

Man as co creators

by composing a figurative hymn of culture, science, and religion. Jesuit paleontologist Teilhard de Chardin's *The Future of Man* (1964) undergoes a metamorphosis into the future of God, while insights from depth psychology contribute to the emergence of a world religion incorporating a transformed Christianity during the third millennium. Murray Stein in his book, *Jung's Treatment of Christianity: The Psychotherapy of a Religious Tradition*, wrote that the evolution of such a nontribal and universal religion might take an estimated six hundred years (1986, 179–194).

In addition to those to whose published work I have already referred, I must acknowledge my indebtedness to theologian Hans Küng, author of *The Beginning of All Things: Science and Religion* (2007), and Anglican priest and physicist John Polkinghorne, author of *Exploring Reality: The Intertwining of Science and Religion* (2006). The emphasis upon the dichotomies of the temporal and eternal and of mind and matter, particularly when considered from the dual perspectives of quantum physics and depth psychology, is to the best of my knowledge an approach to an evolving theology that has been neglected to date. This book attempts to address this neglect, especially in presenting a view of the numinous from the dual perspectives of physics and depth psychology. Finally, the courageous pursuit of truth rather than intemperate bigotry might prove to be a fruitful form of dialogue between sincere skeptics and atheists, on the one hand, and those who experience themselves as religious, on the other.

INTRODUCTION

It is paradoxical perhaps that, in a supposedly post-Enlightenment era of secularism, works either critical of or presenting alternative theological visions to those of religious orthodoxy so frequently become best sellers. Even if God is not dead for the estimated 1.1 billion Roman Catholics, a nearly equal number of Muslims, and hundreds of millions of Anglicans, Protestants, and members of other faiths who currently inhabit the earth, religion could appear to have been dealt potentially mortal blows by science and positivist philosophy alike. Richard Dawkins's book *The God Delusion* (2006) is simply one best-selling example among many that attempts to complete the secular project of deicide while deriding as delusional the experience of the numinous in Western societies where the once great cathedrals may seem destined to become the empty tombs of God.

As a topic in cultural discourse, however, religion is far from dead, nor have the cathedrals collapsed in the face of either the philosophy of metaphysical materialism or the doctrine of mortality as extinction of the self. As Archbishop of Canterbury Rowan Williams is reported to have said, "Richard Dawkins and other apostles of antireligious sentiment are oversimplifying complex issues while missing the point about what theists believe" ("Williams Questions Dawkins' Critical Thinking," 2007, n.p.). C. G. Jung described atheism as a stupid error and a product of intellectual mediocrity, and he consistently referred to God as a psychic fact and as an archetype of a cosmic and timeless nature, for instance, in "Psychology and Religion" (1940) and *Aion* (1951).

I shall argue that eminent skeptics are still trying to rid the world of a concept of God that was already dying in the seventeenth century as a consequence of Newton's discoveries in physics. God and numinous experience—what Archbishop Williams refers to as the "eternal and unconditioned" reality—cannot be strangled by the space and time coordinates of classical physics (I will have more to say about timelessness and whether mind is destructible in later chapters of this book). Physicist and Nobel laureate Erwin Schrödinger wryly commented that a personal God was not to be discovered in a scientific worldview from which anything of this nature had been removed by definition.

For secular humanists, atheism is less a working empirical hypothesis than a quasi-religious, materialistic doctrine. The death of God is to be justified and hastened by emotive rhetoric about ecclesiastical scandals, the association of religion with superstition and intellectual stupefaction, and, where expedient, arguments that selectively distort the positions of some of the greatest names in science, including Erwin Schrödinger and C. G. Jung, while ignoring the self-acknowledged mysticism of others, such as Alfred Russel Wallace, for instance, who perceived the anomaly of mind in evolution as an issue that could not be simply dismissed. Contributions to the solution of this mystery from a scientific perspective include those of physicists such as Erwin Schrödinger, Wolfgang Pauli, David Bohm, and Roger Penrose.

From a theological perspective, the works of controversial writers such as Bishop John Shelby Spong, author of *Liberating the Gospels* (1996), seem to tap into a reservoir of collective curiosity about the numinous and transcendent that has survived the demise of anthropomorphic concepts of God, depicted in the biblical literalism of evangelical and fundamentalist Christianity. Though perhaps less popular and less well known, the eminent theologian Hans Küng, who was censored by the Vatican for his liberal views, has published accessible texts that present a theology friendly to the scientifically enlightened rather than being phobic or hostile toward science. Küng also embraces the importance of interfaith dialogue and the limitations of an exclusive Judeo-Christian perspective. His most recent work, *The Beginning of All Things* (2007), is a breathtakingly refreshing contribution to efforts to overcome the schism between science and religion, a split that has existed for four hundred years, exacerbated by conservative theologians and by materialistic scientists such as Dawkins and American science writer and skeptic Michael Shermer.

In addition to the more or less esoteric publications of the physicists mentioned above, the perspective of science is also represented by the voluminous works of depth psychologists in a direct line of descent from Sigmund Freud and C. G. Jung and by such neuroscientists as Nobel laureate John Eccles in a book cowritten with philosopher Karl Popper titled *The Self and Its Brain: An Argument for Interactionism* (1986) and Karl Pribram in his paper "Consciousness Reassessed" (2004), published in the interdisciplinary journal *Mind and Matter*. Of the two psychologists, Jung is much better known for his contributions to the understanding of religion than is Freud, who, in spite of his personal atheism, nevertheless respected and collaborated with such theologians as the Lutheran minister Oskar Pfister, with whom he had extensive correspondence.

The present book canvasses this vast literature, addressing the psychophysical or mind/matter problem while arguing that even such advances as functional magnetic resonance imaging (fMRI) and positron emission tomography (PET) in neuroscience, which enhance our knowledge of brain processes, do not necessarily entail the acceptance of an eliminative, materialist framework for understanding mind and consciousness. Eminent neuroscientists Eccles and Pribram, for instance, strongly reject such a posture. Brain imaging techniques do not detect subjective phenomenological states such as those experienced in meditation or moments of inspiration. Nor can consciousness be found by digging into the brain, as Pribram has pithily put it (2004, 11).

These diverse works all attempt to facilitate the human and spiritual quest for understanding and meaning as well as the possibility of a living and personal encounter with something numinous. Given that traditional theology in the twenty-first century sends countless people away empty, seeking answers elsewhere to such ultimate questions as the role of consciousness in the universe, what the nature of a nonanthropomorphic God might be, and whether some form of self-continuity or life after death exists. Beneath the urge to solve the enigma of the psychophysical or mind/matter relationship, there often lurks an even deeper questioning about such existential issues as the existence of God and personal immortality. Jung described this quest in *Modern Man in Search of a Soul* (1933). Hence, there is an extensive market for what I refer to as "packaged spirituality" in various forms and increasing appeal in Western societies for Eastern religions such as Tibetan Buddhism which seem to offer a mystical pathway to enlightenment or encounter with the numinous. Jung's individuation process in psychotherapy implied integrating the God archetype and timeless dimensions of the Self into conscious awareness.

These themes carrying us into nonmathematical and accessible accounts of ideas from disciplines as diverse as quantum physics, evolutionary biology, neuroscience, and depth psychology. After considering the case against God being prosecuted by skeptics like

Dawkins in the court of popular appeal, I present an argument for the defense and a critique of what I refer to as the religion of metaphysical materialism, which seems to me to be a menace to the future of humanity and of all life on earth. My argument concludes with an outline of scientific contributions to the possible evolution of a theology for the third millennium.

Unfortunately, contemporary theology, with the notable exception of writers such as Spong, Küng, and John Polkinghorne, remains in a state of schism from science while holding onto a static, pre-Copernican view of the world. The new theology will not be that expressed in the revival of religious fundamentalism with its regression to biblical literalism and antiscientific evangelizing with such doctrines as that of "intelligent design." In Australia, this regressive system of thought is tangibly represented in Hillsong Church, a Pentecostal megachurch, while in the United States it is found in the resurgence of the religious right and evangelical Christianity with its doctrine of intelligent design of the universe by a creator God external to it.

The problems of mind, consciousness, and cultural evolution need to be addressed by a theology that is illuminated not only by post-quantum physics but also by cognitive neuroscience and depth psychology. Küng and Polkinghorne only touch upon these disciplines in their texts. The current book is an attempt to fill this gap, arguing that the complementarity of mind and matter and the concept of timelessness in depth psychology as well as physics are vital to theology and to a scientific understanding of the role of humankind in the future evolution of God. It explores the collaboration between Jung and Pauli in integrating analytical psychology and quantum physics while extending Jung's argument that "God" needs to be understood in psychological terms in order to address the needs of contemporary society.

In contemplating the archetypes as cosmic ordering and regulating principles, I propose that a numinous dimension is implicit in the evolutionary process itself.

I now turn to the challenge of dispelling delusions about God and a future theology in which the schism between science and religion is overcome and the arrow of time does not necessarily deal a mortal blow to its creator!

CHAPTER 1

The Case against God

Richard Dawkins is not the first to argue an apparently compelling case for the proposition of a "God delusion." Sir Isaac Newton is said to have become depressed when he concluded that the elegant mathematical laws of his mechanistic universe had dispensed with the need for an external God to set the clockwork in motion. Even the more sophisticated notion of God as the *prima causa* or first cause, most notably introduced by medieval theologian Thomas Aquinas, became superfluous in a universe bound by strict deterministic causality and in which gravity replaced spirit. However, perhaps, in a subtle sense, Newton himself had replaced God as an external, anthropomorphic designer or clockmaker with the status of an omniscient observer of bodies both celestial and worldly whose influence could be discerned in elegantly beautiful mathematical equations. The eighteenth-century Roman Catholic poet Alexander Pope believed in the existence of a God who presided over a universe that functioned precisely as a cosmic clockwork mechanism. His admiration for Newton is expressed in his epitaph, "Intended for Sir Isaac Newton, in Westminster Abbey" (1735), "Nature and Nature's laws lay hid in night; God said let Newton be and all was Light."

The equations described in Newton's *Principia* were not simply a rapturously beautiful mathematical model of material bodies in motion. To Newton, they were that reality, so that the inconvenient question of the inspiration or source of such equations did not need to be asked. A universe explained with Newton's classical equations was one that permitted nothing personal, including an anthropomorphic God, to be discovered within the defined coordinates of space and time. The human observer was a spectator rather than an actor in the drama of cosmology. It was not until the rise of quantum mechanics in the twentieth century that the issue of the role of mind and consciousness (or the personal equation) of the observer in the experiment could no longer be overlooked. In this chapter I shall begin to explore the proposition that any complete theory of evolution and cosmology must be capable of explaining the emergence of mind and consciousness.

The anthropomorphic God, who had become terminally ill as a result of the machinations of Newton, received another, potentially mortal, blow from Charles Darwin in 1859 with the publication of *On the Origin of Species*. Darwin's notion of the natural selection of chance variations in life forms for adaptation and survival in constantly changing environments provided an appealing scientific explanation for the emergence of species, including Homo sapiens. This thesis disposed of the need to posit a divine designer or creator of living organisms, human beings having evolved from ancestors in the animal world, most notably, their closest prehominid and primate cousins. The idea of a direct line of descent aroused the opposition of the religious establishment because it contradicted the theological doctrine, based upon Genesis, that God had created the species separately and subordinate to humans, who had been made directly in His own image. This is the creation myth depicted in its pristine glory by Michelangelo on the Sistine Chapel ceiling in Rome.

Darwin and his co-discoverer Wallace had yet to specify the mechanisms of the "chance" variations naturally selected. These would be elucidated later by Abbot Gregor Mendel, father of the theory of inheritance in the nineteenth century, and by James Watson and Francis Crick with the publication of their discovery of DNA in 1953. The anomaly of the role of mind in evolution, which Wallace found troubling for Darwin's theory, remained unresolved. Thomas Kuhn, author of *The Structure of Scientific Revolutions* (1996), has defined *anomaly* as a phenomenon or paradox resistant to explanation within a particular scientific theory, such as the problem of the planets encountered by Copernicus which resulted in a revolution in astronomy in the Renaissance.

Strongly influenced by the mechanistic science of the nineteenth century and by Darwin's theory of evolution, Sigmund Freud, father of psychoanalysis, considered the traditional theological concept of God to be a collective delusion exposing what he saw as the narcissism implicit in the view that humanity stood at the center of all things in creation. Like Narcissus in Ovid's myth, humankind seemed to Freud to be absorbed in the grandeur of its own reflection, while the need for God was rooted in an infantile and wish-fulfilling denial of the reality of death.

Part of Freud's project, outlined in such books as *The Future of an Illusion* (1927) and *Moses and Monotheism* (1939), was to rid humankind of this type of collective pathology in order to permit the triumph of science and reason over superstition and irrationality. In *The Future of an Illusion*, Freud inverted the Genesis story by asserting that man created God in his own image. In other words, God was to be understood as nothing but an anthropomorphic projection of the image of an omnipotent and omniscient patriarchal father onto the inanimate universe. According to Freud it was as difficult for the human ego to conceive of its own extinction as to accept that it once had a beginning. Freud viewed religion as inimical to scientific understanding and progress, although he viewed religious art as part of humankind's cultural achievement, which he admired. Like dream symbolism, Freud discerned in artistic masterpieces expressions of the unconscious complexes and mental mechanisms he postulated as well as the archaic legacy of the evolutionary past of humankind.

Dawkins's notion of a God delusion probably has unconscious roots in the seminal thinking of Freud about the origins of religious belief systems and the anthropomorphic concept of God. Irrespective of this, given the banishment of metaphysics and theology from science and contemporary philosophy, Dawkins could appear to be demolishing a largely straw man argument, attempting to commit deicide at a time when the death of God is already on its way to becoming an accomplished historical fact, at least in "enlightened" secular and Western societies, except perhaps, for the resurgence of religious fundamentalism in Western democracies.

Fundamentalism is literalism in interpreting the scriptures of any religious tradition as history rather than as mythology and metaphor expressing universal or archetypal themes of timeless significance for humankind's understanding of its origins, future destiny, and significance in cosmology. In a fundamentalist approach the historical existence of such spiritual figures as Moses, Christ, and Mohammed and the infallibility of teachings attributed to them are emphasized at the expense of the symbolic meaning of their roles as archetypal deliverers, heroes, and saviors for their collective peoples.

Archetypal and symbolic meaning tends to be eclipsed by an obsession with the literal truth of the scriptures. The collective projection of numinous qualities onto such figures has resulted in religious wars evoked when rival traditions are demonized as embodying shadow attributes. When God becomes human or delivers a message through a prophet, the figurative light associated with the "chosen" figure casts competitors and their followers into collective darkness. I shall have much more to say about religious archetypes in chapter 4.

Former president George Bush, for example, could be viewed as a theocrat whose "conversations with God" convinced him to strike Iraq with the assistance of the so-called "coalition of the willing" and to formulate his axis of evil in anticipation of further crusades. I find Dawkins's arguments against the primitive and archaic version of fundamentalist theism (with its patriarchal father God), which political conservatives embrace to further their amoral and exploitive ends, thoroughly convincing.

Scientific research, intellectual freedom, and philosopher Karl Popper's ideal of the open society need to be defended against such irrationality, as well as kept from the slippery slope toward totalitarianism. The case against God needs to be prosecuted vigorously against fundamentalist systems of religious thought, just as it does, I shall argue, against the religion of materialism, which is a menace to authentic spirituality and the future of humanity alike.

However, whether it is still possible to argue a case for a concept of the numinous or for God that is beyond the criticism of skeptics like Dawkins yet also compatible with science is the primary question addressed by this book. The prosecution of the case against the absurdities and excesses of religious fundamentalism need not necessarily result in the rejection of humankind's spiritual search for meaning and transcendence. The thesis here advanced is that Dawkins is stuck in a largely classical scientific view of the universe and of evolution that is outdated and which explains nothing at all about the role of consciousness in evolving culture, including science and religion.

Recent applications of quantum mechanics and information theory to biosystems, for example, those outlined by physicist Koichiro Matsuno (2000), have adopted an internalist ecological perspective on such phenomena as adaptive (directed) mutation in microorganisms, as well as the emergent evolutionary phenomena of life and consciousness. I shall take up these topics and discuss them further in chapters 2 and 3. From this perspective biosystems appear to have arrived at a form of quantum computing in advance of humankind and become capable of monitoring their own internal informational states or software.

Far from being delusional or merely filling gaps in knowledge, some concept of God may be vital to the cultural evolution of humankind as well as the future of life on earth, as the Jesuit priest and palaeontologist Teilhard de Chardin clearly envisioned in his book *The Phenomenon of Man* (1959), in which the emergence of the noosphere, or envelope of consciousness surrounding the world, and human responsibility for evolution are described. The mystical connotations of such concepts can be difficult for zealous skeptics to swallow. Dawkins savagely attacked Teilhard de Chardin for gross "self-deception" when he agrees with the immunologist Peter Medawar's statement about Teilhard's book, that "its author can be excused of dishonesty only on the grounds that before deceiving others, he has taken great pains to deceive himself" (2006, 154). By contrast, the eminent humanist and biologist Julian Huxley praised the work in his introduction to *The Phenomenon of Man*. Huxley wrote, "He has both clarified and unified our vision of reality.... The religiously minded can no longer turn their backs on the natural world or seek escape from imperfection in a supernatural world. Nor can the materialistically minded deny importance to spiritual experience and religious feeling" (Teilhard de Chardin 1959, 26). At the beginning of his introduction, Huxley describes Teilhard as "a very remarkable man, at the same time a Jesuit father and a distinguished palaeontologist.... He has effected a threefold synthesis of the material world and the physical world with the world of mind and spirit" (ibid., 1).

Evolution, Mind, and Matter

Physicist Wolfgang Pauli won the Nobel Prize for his formulation of the exclusion principle which explained the complex ordering of the elements on the periodic table. Having collaborated with depth psychologist C. G. Jung concerning the role of the "personal equation"—the mind of the observer in quantum experiments—Pauli referred to the psychophysical problem as "the most challenging of our time" and the Copenhagen interpretation of quantum mechanics as an insight into "a world which is characterized by the complementarity of spirit and matter and of religion and science," as noted by the late high-energy physicist Kalervo Laurikainen (1988, xv). With Jung, Pauli regarded the archetypes of the collective unconscious as cosmic ordering and regulating principles that determined the nature of patterned information even in inanimate matter, while the origins of scientific theories were in the human psyche, especially the unconscious. I shall discuss Pauli's ideas in considerable detail in chapter 3.

Solving the psychophysical problem will entail, I shall argue, the admission of a nontrivial God concept that is neither an animistic projection nor personified and clothed in parental garments, as is the case with the anthropomorphic image of God in traditional theology. Jung believed that it is the energy of the God archetype in conjunction with the qualities of omnipotence and omniscience imputed to the parents during childhood, which results in such anthropomorphism. Infants, like primitive peoples, evolve through an animistic stage that involves the personification of nature; during this stage phenomena such as mountains and storms are thought to be manifestations of the divine. A tendency to project mental qualities onto the heavens was not lost on Shakespeare, who wrote in his play *Julius Caesar* a line attributed to Cassius, "The fault, dear Brutus, is not in our stars but in ourselves that we are underlings" (line 140).

Put succinctly, the question of the existence of God lies at the heart of the psychophysical or mind/matter problem. Matter, of course, includes the substance of the human brain, which stands at the summit of biological evolution in terms of complexity, order, and central or self-organization. The God hypothesis is no less plausible, I shall argue, than the anthropic principle, which is favored by Dawkins in his explanation of the cosmological conditions necessary for the existence of complex life forms, including those which have evolved a consciousness capable of explaining their own origins and the origins of the universe itself. Dawkins treatment of the explanatory power of the anthropic principle is outlined in his book *The God Delusion* (2006, 134–151) in conjunction with a multiverse theory in which at least one universe compatible with the existence of life and sentient beings would occur given sufficient time. His extrapolation of natural selection to cosmology and multiple universes prior to the origins of life seems to me to be both ad hoc and as empirically unsupported as the God hypothesis which he rejects with such militancy. Dawkins argument is addressed only to the anthropomorphic God concept which had become dispensable with both the physics of Newton and Darwin's theory of evolution. Oxford physicist Roger Penrose, in his book *The Road to Reality: A Complete Guide to the Laws of the Universe* (2004), seems to be far less in awe of the alleged explanatory power of the anthropic principle, preferring what he refers to as the weak version rather than the strong form that Dawkins requires to do the heavy work of explanation.

Put more bluntly, Penrose regards the anthropic principle as having an almost trivial role in both cosmology and life, because it simply states the conditions that are required in the universe (such as the value of the so-called strong force being such that the complex elements on the periodic table are possible) for these phenomena to emerge. Physicist Paul Davies, by contrast, in his Templeton Prize–winning book *The Mind of God* (1992), was moved to write of the universe as a "put up job," partly because of the apparently felicitous combination of multiple improbable conditions necessary for the existence of a planet such as Earth, capable of sustaining the origins of life.

Relying upon the anthropic principle as a sufficient explanation not only of the origins of life, but also of such complex organisms as humans, endowed with consciousness and those nonalgorithmic aspects of intelligence expressed in mathematical insights and scientific epiphanies, to which Penrose refers, may really seem to stretch one's credulity. According to Penrose, "consciousness is not some kind of epiphenomenon" (2004, 1033). It is "the phenomenon whereby the universe's very existence is made known" (Penrose 1999, 580). Furthermore, invoking something analogous to Darwin's natural selection in cosmology and prior to the origins of life to explain the existence of at least one universe out of many (or a multiverse) in which such phenomena emerge purely as a result of random variations seems to be very close to substituting a religion of chance for the God hypothesis.

And yet this is the precise argument that Dawkins adduces as more economical than the "extravagant" introduction of God into the picture (2006, 146). Perhaps Jung had a point when he suggested in "Psychology and Religion" that "atheism is a stupid error" (1940, 82).

Even if one stays with the spectacular display of mental gymnastics produced by Dawkins to keep God out of the picture and concedes some validity to the argument that he (and other skeptics) have put forth, other reasons exist for entertaining some form of God hypothesis, and it is to these ideas that I shall now turn.

If, as physicist David Bohm has suggested, even the quantum level can be thought to have a primitive mindlike quality as a result of "active information," though consistent with the theory of emergent evolution, devoid of consciousness, then crude materialism which denies the mental is erroneous. This error becomes even more egregious when considering the possibility that quantum computing and information processing might have fast-tracked the beginnings of life, for instance, in the form of self-replicating molecules such as RNA.

However, to speak of cosmic ordering and regulating principles, as Pauli did, and of mind as active information, existing prior to the emergence of consciousness, might just as well be another language for talking about God "implicate" in matter, though stripped of anthropomorphic attributes. Bohm, I believe, came close to such a notion in his book *Wholeness and the Implicate Order* (1980). In contrast to Dawkins's contemptuous critique of the "illusion of design" in nature, we are confronted with forms of active information that are as real as the software in our own personal computers!

The computational parallelism characteristic of quantum computing attributed to biosystems by some eminent physicists are far from illusory, as my treatment of directed or adaptive mutation in chapter 3 will demonstrate.

Perspectives on the Psychophysical Problem

The issue of the existence of God seems to be entangled with and part of the psychophysical problem, so before proceeding further with scientific argument, I shall outline some relevant philosophical perspectives in a brief diversion into the history and philosophy of the psychophysical or mind/body problem. Currently, an entire journal, *Mind and Matter* (www.mindmatter.de), is devoted to contributions to understanding the issue, from disciplines as diverse as cognitive neuroscience, depth psychology, and quantum mechanics. I begin with metaphysical materialism, which has no place for predicating the attribute of existence to God or for discovering anything either personal or numinous within the classical coordinates of space and time. Paradoxically perhaps, materialism has at least an unconscious, quasi-religious or numinous quality for devoted skeptics because it is a doctrine about nature rather than being an explanation of it.

This philosophical position asserts that the entire fabric and reality of the universe can be explained by purely material or physical processes. It is technically a metaphysical proposition because it is an assertion that transcends any reality that can be predicated both to exist and to be susceptible to empirical observation. It consists of propositions about the cosmos that do not satisfy the falsifiability criterion of science as outlined, for example, by Popper (1972). In other words, no possible observations can be made that would demonstrate their falsity. The proposition is no less metaphysical than the more obvious position of monist idealism, which asserts that the whole of reality consists of mind or ideas, a position also known as solipsism.

By contrast, the assumption that consciousness permeates the universe and that somehow everything is endowed with this quality is known as panpsychism. One major objection to panpsychism is that it imputes consciousness to forms and stages in the evolution of matter which could have sustained neither life nor consciousness, for instance, the heat of the early universe. It denies the well-established theory of emergent evolution whereby life and consciousness only appear when matter has reached a critical degree of complexity, order, and self-organization.

As mentioned above, Pauli's exclusion principle explains the ordering of elements on the periodic table into more complex ones. The fallacy of panpsychism is avoided if, at the quantum level, mind is regarded as active information, yet devoid of consciousness, as suggested by physicist Basil Hiley (Hiley and Pylkkänen 2005), who was a colleague of David Bohm. This formulation is compatible with the theory of emergent evolution.

The philosophical position referred to as reductionism assumes two primary forms. One is the reduction of all reality to material processes while denying the predicate of existence to mental phenomena. The other is idealism, which reduces reality to mind or Platonic ideas while viewing matter as an illusion. Both forms of reductionism maintain the Cartesian split of reality into mind and matter or result in some form of dualist interactionism, parallelism, or epiphenomenalism (for example, mind is just an epiphenomenal by-product of brain processes, without causal efficacy). The dual aspect positions do not entail such reductions of reality into either the mental or the physical.

Dualist interactionism derives from the seventeenth-century philosophy of René Descartes, though the question of how mind could affect matter remained a mystery, one that could be ignored, while the classical physics of Newton was thought to provide a comprehensive if not sufficient set of explanations for the behavior of the cosmos. Concepts of the mental as attributes of the human observer became important with the rise of quantum physics during the 1920s, most notably perhaps in the Copenhagen interpretation of quantum theory. Niels Bohr's notion of complementarity, Pauli's concept of statistical causality, and Werner Heisenberg's uncertainty principle raised questions about the possible relevance and causal significance of mind and the personal equation in the experimental situation.

Thus, developments in quantum physics disposed of the Newtonian absolutes with respect to causality and determinism while opening a door for reconsideration of the observer's consciousness, as well as intention and free will. Dualist interactionism proposes that rather than existing in parallel, mind and matter interact, with the implication of downward as well as upward causality and the possibility of mind acting upon matter, in particular, that of the brain.

Popper and neuroscientist and Nobel laureate John Eccles embraced this position in their book *The Self and Its Brain: An Argument for Interactionism* (1983), and it currently appears to be favored by Penrose. Penrose writes of nonalgorithmic aspects of mental functioning and of a realm of mathematical and scientific insight independent of the brain, while postulating that consciousness and the nonalgorithmic aspects of thought and intelligence are associated with quantum gravity–induced collapses in the wave function which result in active quantum information. Hiley and Pylkkänen, in their paper "Can Mind Affect Matter Via Active Information" (2005), provide an elaborate outline of these processes and the notion of a "mind field," the nature of which is discussed in chapter 3.

Perhaps the most plausible position on the psychophysical (mind/ matter) problem is that of complementarity, a term originally coined by Bohr. This dual aspect monist hypothesis was also adopted by Bohm and Pauli. Complementarity enables the same reality, whether expressed as subatomic particles or subtle brain processes, to be viewed from two equally valid and real perspectives. Bohm used the analogy of a magnet which has both north and south poles while remaining a unitary entity.

Another example of a dual aspect monist position has been proposed by Hans Primas (2003) in his "disentanglement" of two domains of time into the "tensed" time (having past, present, and future) of nonmaterial processes and mental events and what he refers to as the "tenseless" time of matter and physical energy. Both of these domains result from breaking the symmetry of a primordial, timeless reality, the significance of which I shall discuss further in chapters 3 and 6.

Similarly, neuroscientist Karl Pribram begins with what he refers to as "prespacetime" in his paper, *"Consciousness Reassessed"* (2004), in which he argues that both mind and matter have a common ontological root referred to as a "holoflux," similar in meaning to Bohm's "holo-movement." This ontological foundation transcends spacetime.

A brief quotation from Pribram's contribution will suffice to introduce the concepts. He writes, "Thinking and its communication are the consequence of a neg-entropic forming of flux, its information" (2004, 13). Alluding to Hiley's work, Pribram understands information as putting form into process (the significance of this idea will hopefully become clearer when we explore these contributions in chapters 2 and 3). Negentropy, of course, means creating order.

I have provided this detour into the philosophical treatment of the psychophysical problem because Dawkins's ejection of God from the domain of science as a "delusion" implies the epistemology of metaphysical materialism. Such ousting also means either rejecting or grotesquely distorting the theory of emergent evolution. It is to this embarrassing and inconvenient truth that I now turn in revisiting the scientific understanding of evolution. An evolutionary theory that explains mind and consciousness and is compatible with religion and a third millennium theology could provide a rebuttal of the arguments adduced in support of the doctrine of metaphysical materialism.

Evolution Revisited

Dawkins's evolutionary credo seems to be that, given enough time, even highly improbable and complex life forms will occur as a result of purely random mutations, thriving as a result of natural selection in those environments to which they are adapted for survival. His metaphor for this thesis is a 747 aircraft being assembled out of scrap metal by a hurricane, again given that enough time has elapsed. This illustration of the natural selection of purely chance events is simply a variation of the familiar monkey writing a Shakespeare play by randomly hitting the keys of a typewriter. Dawkins relies on the strong version of the anthropic principle to account for the occurrence of all the cosmic events and conditions necessary for the appearance of life even in its complex forms, to do the heavy lifting of providing a compelling explanation of the emergence of life, humanity, and consciousness in the universe. The weak form described, for instance, by Penrose simply specifies the nature and conditions (including the six fundamental constants of physics) that must be present in a universe for life and eventually human beings to emerge. It does not purport to be a causal explanation in terms of necessity and sufficiency of conditions. The unthinkable alternative to skeptics is the so-called God hypothesis.

This distinction between the weak and strong versions of the anthropic principle is not trivial for Dawkins, because he wishes to contrast the principle with the "highly improbable" existence of God as an explanation of cosmology, evolution, and the ascent of humanity. Dawkins writes, "God, or any intelligent, decision-taking, calculating agent, would have to be highly improbable in the very same statistical sense as the entities he is supposed to explain" (2006, 147). Again, Dawkins is referring to an external, anthropomorphic intelligently designing God. He has cleverly set up a dichotomy between a scientifically respectable extension of the anthropic principle (with the existence of God so improbable as to be absurd) and the obviously disreputable doctrine of intelligent design. I assume that Dawkins would have no objections to refuting this creationist doctrine as unfalsifiable and hence pseudoscientific, even if he would be less comfortable applying the falsifiability criterion to his own use of the anthropic principle buttressed by the multiverse theory as an explanatory hypothesis.

While criticizing Davies for accepting the Templeton Prize for his book *The Mind of God* (1992) in the comment, "for which he was rewarded with the Templeton Prize (a very large sum of money given annually by the Templeton Foundation usually to a scientist who is prepared to say something nice about religion" [2006, 19], Dawkins seems to have no scruple about relying on the anthropic principle in a way that comes close to being a tautology or *petitio principii* [circular reasoning]—inventing a term, then using it vacuously as an explanation of itself).

In writing as a devout disciple of orthodox neo-Darwinism, arguing the case that the appearance or "illusion" of design in evolution can be explained by the principle of the natural selection of random mutations alone, I believe that Dawkins commits two cardinal errors. The first is to minimize the significance of the theory of emergent evolution and the evidence supporting it. The second is his casuistic treatment of cultural evolution, consciousness, and mind with a heavy reliance on the meme construct to do the work of explaining almost everything from religion to science and higher mathematics.

Dawkins apparently is not aware that the strict neo-Darwinian paradigm may be collapsing under the weight of experimental evidence demonstrating adaptive or directed mutation in microorganisms, for example, and speculation that the genetic code may need to be construed as a quantum one. McFadden and Al-Khalili provide experimental evidence for such nonrandom mutation in their paper titled, "A Quantum Mechanical Model of Adaptive Mutation" (1999). Mutation is now being considered a result of quantum fluctuations, as Schrödinger (1992) suggested, not merely the result of the effects of mutagens in the external environment. This is an internalist perspective, in contradistinction to the purely externalist perspective postulated by traditional neo-Darwinism.

The Concept of Emergence

The theory of emergent evolution and its implications for the God delusion seem to be an article of quasi-religious faith for Dawkins and his skeptical colleagues. The evolution of matter is an epic story of ever-increasing states of complexity, order, and central organization with the emergence of the most primitive of life forms an estimated four billion years ago. These may have been simple self-replicators like RNA. Biological complexity is *information based* and yet, according to Davies (2004), for instance, simple calculation reveals that it would take much longer than the entire age of the universe for even a single protein to form by chance. Thus, the classical chance hypothesis of the origins or emergence of life may turn out to be as implausible as it is improbable.

By a simple extension of logic, the traditional neo-Darwinian explanation of the origin of species, including human beings, may also be as implausible as it is improbable. If quantum mechanics or computing had fast-tracked matter to life on the basis of the type of computational parallelism referred to by Richard Feynman (1986) in his discussion of quantum computing twenty years ago, then the concept of natural selection would need to be extended to explain the origins of life as well as species variation once living organisms exist. As McFadden and Al-Khalili (1999) have intimated, conceptualizing the genetic code as a quantum code would permit the vastly enhanced computational speed made possible through superpositions of multiple mutated and nonmutated states, for example, in microorganisms such as the mycobacterium tuberculosis which his research group has studied.

Quantum computing would also greatly accelerate the process of mutation, whereby new species or variations appear. Even at the level of microorganisms, self-organization and the internal processing of information are evident. If, as I shall argue later, biosystems have "discovered" quantum information processing (computing) ahead of humans, one no longer need be especially impressed by any "illusion of design" as Dawkins would have it (2006, 157–158). It is simply not possible to speak of the "software" of even the informational molecules, RNA and DNA, without concluding that species variation is as much a result of internal "programming" as external environmental factors impinging upon species.

Hiley and Pylkkänen (2005) designate active information as a form of rudimentary mind, though without consciousness. As far as the higher mental aspects of consciousness are concerned, meaning is to be found in the complexity of patterns of information rather than in simple bits, an idea also found in the work of Pribram.

Suffice it to say here that Dawkins passes over such inconvenient truths in silence, not only because they undermine his traditional form of evolutionary thinking, but also perhaps because they can be construed as dangerously close to a concept of God that is *not* outside of natural science. Such a concept of a numinous dimension of the universe may actually emerge from a science of evolution informed by postclassical quantum physics. Somewhat humorously perhaps, one might ask whether God is some form of super quantum computer such that humans are destined to discover what *already exists in nature*. Could such a device serve as a better metaphor for God than the notion of an external cosmic designer?

The concept of emergent evolution entails the emergence of increasingly complex, ordered, and self-organized forms of matter along an arrow of time characteristic of an expanding universe. It also implies that such phenomena as life and consciousness could not be predicted from a knowledge of prior states alone, such as the so-called primordial soup from which life is supposed to have emerged. Life theoretically could have remained at the simple self-replicator or microorganism level without evolving further. That it did is one of the unsolved mysteries of science, although Dawkins appears to perceive no such enigma or mystery to be solved at all. Another feature of emergent evolution is that it implies a nonreductionist framework of scientific understanding so that, for instance, the laws of sociology and biology cannot be reduced to those of classical physics. Skeptics like Dawkins seem to feel uncomfortable with consciousness and mentalism precisely because such phenomena resist crude forms of materialist reductionism. To such thinkers, wielding Occam's razor to eliminate mind might well seem to be consistent with the principle of parsimony in science, one which would also acknowledge the futility of digging into the brain to find consciousness!

Most alarming to skeptics devoted to the religion of materialism, in which chance determination is an article of faith, would be the notion that language and culture might be construed as artifacts of mind which program the brain as an organ of consciousness. Reflection in conscious thought creates culture, including such theoretical edifices as Darwin's formulation of natural selection. In accordance with the idea of emergence, it is only with the wisdom of hindsight that the life-forms and organizations that exist today seem to be somehow inevitable. Yet this very inevitability is itself an illusion predicated on the absence of awareness that what may evolve in the future cannot easily be envisioned today. Even scientific prediction of future events is probabilistic, and before the rise of science, Teilhard de Chardin's "future of man" would have been very misty indeed.

The Future of an Illusion

Consider Dawkins's notion that the illusion of design in nature is nothing more than a result of natural selection operating over a suitably lengthy time interval, say, four billion years for the evolution of increasingly complex life-forms or species. Even in the absence of a well-supported empirical account of how life began, this notion is empirically meaningless without an evidence-based explanatory crane supporting an argument for how life began. In one sense, his ostensibly new argument directed against intelligent design is old wine in new skins. It is one of many variations on the theme of dismissing the existence of God by dispelling the illusion of design either in species diversity and their fit to changing environments to which they are adapted or in apparently miraculous or perfectly conceived organs such as the human eye.

For the moment, I shall leave aside other sorts of "miracles," such as those referred to by Penrose (2004) in his discussion of surprising and extremely beautiful mathematical insights and solutions that seem to be epiphanies to those who just happen to stumble upon them consciously. I shall also defer a discussion of such eureka moments in scientific experience as those that led to the formulation of Kekulé's benzene ring theory in chemistry, Einstein's special relativity theory, or even the theory of evolution itself. All of these phenomena entail deploying mind and a nonepiphenomenal consciousness within an emergent evolutionary framework.

The anomaly of the emergence of the human mind remains as much a scandal for strict neo-Darwinism today as it did when Wallace first formulated it. As I have already hinted, the concept of mind as active information at the quantum level is potentially even more of an embarrassment, especially when it is applied to mutation as a possible determinant of new species that will be discovered by natural selection, for example, in the directed or adaptive mutations reported by McFadden and Al-Khalili and others.

In a largely trivial sense, Dawkins is right in his treatment of the application of intelligent design doctrine to the origin of species. Romantic poet William Blake's "Tyger, Tyger, burning bright, in the forests of the night," in its "fearful symmetry," can seem to be fortuitously designed for its ecological niche and available food supplies, when in reality it is simply an example of Tennyson's "nature red in tooth and claw" and a product of natural selection. Neo-Darwinism provides a perfectly plausible explanation of this phenomenon, which was a source of such poetic awe to Blake in his romantic mysticism or pantheism.

Dawkins's attack upon the illusions used to support intelligent design, however, is relevant only to a concept of God that was already dying in the wake of Newton and pronounced dead by the end of the nineteenth century. As Nietzsche put it, the churches had become "the tombs of God." Such illusions have no more future in the twenty-first century than they did in the first fifty years after publication of *On the Origin of Species*. In a sense, Dawkins's exhumation of the illusionist argument is little more than a construct or a rhetorical prop, the sole purpose of which seems to be that of supporting his case for the existence of a collective God delusion. This notion has no future except perhaps among undergraduate iconoclasts looking for something to debunk in order to demonstrate intellectual prowess to their professors. If such academics also happen to be devotees of the religion of materialism, they can hope for their published works to become best sellers in a market where the invisible hand of natural selection favors books debunking orthodox religion and organizations like the Templeton Foundation.

It may be the scientism espoused by religious materialists that is the illusion without a future, not a sense of spirituality and the numinous compatible with science. My central thesis, however, encompasses the emergence and role of mind and consciousness in evolution while exploring developments at the frontiers of science that may have implications for religion and a theology for the third millennium. If as Bohm, for instance, has suggested, the "universe has created in us a mirror to reflect upon itself" (2002, 389), then an account of evolution that glosses over quantum information theory, neuroscience, and depth psychology is itself an exercise in obscurantism and self-deception, one which conceals an implicate order, a cosmic ordering principle, or a numinous face as if beneath a veil.

It is one task of this book to dispel the "cloud of intellectual fog" to which Pauli referred in relation to the psychophysical problem and, in particular, to the one-sided materialism in the West which overlooked or repressed the personal equation or "inner state of the human observer," so that "the aftereffects of observation which were ignored would still enter the picture as atomic bombs and general anxiety—the Oppenheimer case" (Laurikainen 1988, 224–226). Pauli was referring to the consequences of repressing the psyche (spirit) in physics and the vengeful return of repressed spirit in such forms as the destructive power of atomic bombs. Humanity may already be experiencing this revenge in the form of globally salient problems that threaten the ultimate survival of the species, the solutions of which will necessitate an awakening to the meaning of their emergence and the discovery of the divine potential of becoming wholly and fully human.

Global Summonses

Humankind is already confronting major challenges to its future survival. Teilhard de Chardin predicted that these would act as symbolic "summonses" to the unanimization of the species, that is, to the emergence of a geopolitical holism and collective consciousness of the sacredness of the earth which gives us life, while being indispensable for the sustenance of future generations. In a sense, Teilhard's voice may turn out to have been prophetic even if he could not envision in his time the precise form these summonses would take when presented to his noosphere.

Dawkins is scathing in his criticism of Teilhard de Chardin, while lacking compassion for a courageous visionary who was unjustly condemned, persecuted, and silenced by the Catholic Church (2006, 154). It was heroic of Teilhard to defend the theory of evolution in the face of pre-Vatican II Catholicism. As Hans Küng pointed out, Teilhard was subjected to *damnatio memoriae* (erasure of his memory) by banning and forbidding the sale of his writings as well as the teaching of his work, even in science (2007, 97–102). However, Dawkins seems to have missed something of crucial significance in Teilhard's later writing, something perhaps more comprehensible for humankind today in a world confronting the challenges of global warming and pandemics such as HIV/AIDS, tuberculosis, and avian influenza.

What Dawkins is missing is precisely the notion of a transcendent implicate order, archetypal cosmic ordering and regulating principles discernable in inanimate matter, in evolving life, and in the emergence of humanity as Bohm's mirror, created by the universe to reflect upon itself. Both Pauli and Bohm move away from considering the consciousness or mind of the individual observer to contemplating not only the collective consciousness of humanity but also a Mind that extends infinitely beyond this psyche.

The implication is of a form of mind or active information that transcends the finiteness of the human ego and yet somehow encompasses the universe itself. In light of such critiques of theism as those provided by Dawkins and a long line of illustrious intellectual ancestors before him, including such positivist philosophers as Bertrand Russell and his pupil Ludwig Wittgenstein who, in his *Tractatus* (1922), nevertheless sensed mystery in the discovery that there is "something rather than nothing at all," it is important to emphasize the internalist perspective which I am adopting in my argument for a numinous dimension of being.

This is entirely consistent with what Teilhard described as the "within of matter" in *The Phenomenon of Man* (1959). There is no implication here of any external deity somehow installing software or programming patterned information or mathematical order into matter or living organisms, in a manner suggestive of the old God which Newton deposed. What does emerge from matter in the course of evolution is consciousness, culture, and science.

And with it evolves, however subtly, a striving not only for global unity, but also one in which anachronistic forms of tribalism and nationalism are replaced by a sense of reverence toward the earth and toward all of its more than six billion human centers of reflective consciousness. The religion of materialism, consumerism, and totalitarian systems of nationalistic, economic, and political thought continue to obstruct such a *unio mystica* while perpetuating the desacralization of science and humankind.

It is to a more profoundly understood noosphere that the global summonses to which I referred are being delivered. I have suggested, in an essay titled "The Neglected Holocaust" (Todd 2007), that responding to these summonses will require the recognition of a figurative quantum entanglement between the developed and developing worlds, implying a geopolitical holism that transcends the confines of religious tribalism, nationalism, and economic self-interest. It is now time to explicate the nature of these figurative summonses, before considering the many layers of argument for a concept of the numinous revealed to us, paradoxically, by evolution itself.

The "revenge of psyche and spirit," of which Pauli warned and which has been exorcised from science for four hundred years, is now occurring on the basis of the bioterrorism of microorganisms such as HIV. I have argued elsewhere that HIV can be construed as a retroviral messenger with awesome destructive power for humankind especially if its summons to humanity continues to be minimized and its continual mutation into more virulent forms is ignored as a potent threat to global national and economic security, not just in the developing world.

If the prodigious mutation of this and other deadly microorganisms reflects the possible discovery by biosystems of quantum computing in advance of humanity, there may already exist biological systems that represent a threat to humankind's evolutionary dominance or survival. Such systems do not need to know about intelligent design. Their capacity to monitor their own internal quantum information states and to mutate on the basis of quantum mechanical processes would confer upon them an adaptive advantage over humans.

Thus, like the global warming that threatens future generations, HIV and other deadly pathogens represent a challenge and a summons to humanity as a whole. This challenge almost demands unanimization and the transcendence of human divisions rooted in economic and political ideologies and faith traditions. It may also mean a spiritual awakening and transformation of collective consciousness, a rediscovery of something numinous about human existence. Such an evolutionary shift, however, will mean the end of religious fundamentalism, a theme to which I now turn.

CHAPTER 2

Religious Fundamentalism as a Shadow

One major challenge to the survival of humanity is religious fundamentalism in its various guises. These include uncritical belief in the inerrancy of scriptures and credal statements, such as interpreting the Genesis myth as a historical account of cosmology and creation. The presence of such fundamentalism is a summons to humankind to embrace tolerance of religious differences, interfaith dialogue, and world peace as imperatives. As rigid and dogmatic systems of belief in the inerrancy of religious texts, fundamentalisms are tribal rather than universal (or manifestations of the "God archetype" as the source of numinous experience) and tend to be intolerant of differences in faith tradition and are therefore unlikely to be open to such dialogue. In previous historical epochs, religion, while dangerous at times to individuals and groups, was not a threat to species survival. Weapons of mass destruction, biological or nuclear, had not been developed. With their invention comes the potential to sacrifice billions of people on the altar of scriptural literalism and belief in either monotheistic or polytheistic systems of thought. In the twenty-first century, it is chillingly obvious that such technologies can easily be utilized in the name of one or another variety of religious fundamentalism, either to fulfill a vision of Armageddon or to garner power by rationalizing military intervention motivated by control of energy resources. It is in this sense that religious fundamentalism can be seen as a collective manifestation of the collective Jungian shadow archetype.

In his apotheosis of Reason, however, Richard Dawkins, in *The God Delusion* (2006), seems to me to be in some danger of neglecting other irrational motives for wars waged apparently in the name of religion or God. The Roman Empire, for instance, conducted military campaigns for the purposes of power and expansion, subjugating conquered peoples to the Pax Romana while plundering their resources. Devotion to the emperor as a numinous hero figure and to the gods of the Greco-Roman pantheon provided a rationalization for such expansionism.

In the contemporary world, the climate of mutual suspicion and paranoia between the Abrahamic faiths, or religions of the Book, make the possibility of a thermonuclear version of the apocalypse very real. On the basis of collective archetypal projection entire nations can be demonized as part of an "axis of evil" and thus perceived as capable of the most diabolical destructiveness. Because the projection is unconscious, belief in the malevolence of the Other is held with complete conviction, as, for example, during Hitler's Third Reich, the Jewish people were dehumanized as a menace to the state and their extermination as *untermenschen* could be justified with an attitude of moral righteousness and extreme anti-Semitic prejudice.

Terrorist acts in the name of militant forms of Islam are ultimately a Sisyphean exercise in futility motivated by archetypal shadow projections. Religious fundamentalism is a menace not only because it is one cause of wars which are driven by competition for scarce energy resources. It also corrupts the collective "superego" of nations as well as their leaders to such an extent that, without guilt or remorse, mass murder and even genocide can be perpetrated. Having established this point of partial agreement with Dawkins's position, I must draw the reader's attention to another phenomenon which should be distinguished from the manifestations of religious fundamentalism. In doing so I am utilizing the perspectives of Jung's analytical psychology and sociology, which fall outside of Dawkins's explanatory framework.

This is the phenomenon of the almost numinous energy and power that has historically been invested in charismatic leaders who led their people to wars of conquest. Hitler, Stalin, and Chairman Mao, to name three examples, became "archetypal" heroes and saviors for their people who in turn readily committed mass murder and genocide at their command. One could suggest that such leaders were deified or at least venerated in a manner otherwise reserved for supposedly divine beings. Of these three, Stalin and Mao were materialists and atheists, while Hitler, whose childhood background was Catholic, wanted his Reich to be endowed with the glory of the Roman Empire, reviving the pre-Christian zeitgeist of antiquity and enacting his own messianic delusions about being destined to lead an Aryan master race.

Even without invoking religion, such political figures act in such a way as to induce infantile regression in the collective psyche by instilling fear while assuming the role of omnipotent, omniscient, and hence Godlike parents from whom protection from the specter of terrorism and destructiveness is to be sought. Dawkins perceives religion as the root of much of the world's evil, but I think he misses some important points about the ontogenetic and phylogenetic evolutionary origins of religious experience. Even in ostensibly secular or atheistic states, the same sorts of atrocities, wars, and genocides have occurred as those attributed to states acting within religious systems of thought.

Karl Marx dismissed religion as the "opium of the people." However, he probably would have been horrified by the hideous mass murders carried out, for instance, by Stalin and Mao in the name of dialectical materialism, arguably a secular religion of the state. I shall defer further discussion of the roots of religious experience to later chapters, in which I argue that an explanation in terms of the "memetic selection" suggested by Dawkins is largely verbal and insufficient.

The real question to be addressed in this book is whether some concept of the numinous or of God, other than the primitive animistic and anthropomorphic notions characteristic of humankind in its infancy, is either compatible with empirical science or already discernable in science itself. The God of religious fundamentalism was largely killed off by the scientific theories of Newton and Darwin, though Dawkins does not seem to be thoroughly convinced of the success of this particular form of deicide. He seems thoroughly determined to ensure that the assassination of God is completed and the "dangerous" beliefs of fundamentalism are buried beyond any hope of final resurrection. But the end of religious fundamentalism will not eliminate the human quest for the experience of the numinous and for transpersonal meaning in life. It simply means the death of primitive concepts and archaic theologies driven by the animism and anthropocentrism of prescientific periods of human history. The end of religious fundamentalism makes room for the cosmic religious feeling described by such eminent scientists as Einstein, Schrödinger, Pauli, and C. G. Jung, who were not adherents of religious orthodoxy and doctrine although they probably experienced the numinosity of the God archetype in mystical experiences and in moments of mathematical and scientific inspiration (Penrose 1999, 544–545).

Decryption of the enigma of the existence of God may lie in a more profound grasp of the nature of genetic and quantum information theory, particularly as molecular microbiologist Johnjoe McFadden (McFadden and Al-Khalili 1999) and physicists Koichiro Matsuno (2000), Roger Penrose (2004), and Paul Davies (2004) have suggested.

For instance, RNA and DNA molecules may need to be understood in terms that go beyond the traditional genetic code to encompass a quantum code, not just in their "hardware," but in their "software" or informational properties, as Davies has described them. What if mutation is not only vastly accelerated by some form of quantum information processing but also directed or adaptive? What would be the implications of discovering empirically an affirmative answer to Matsuno's question, "Who got there first, biosystems or Richard Feynman" (2000, 39)? For instance, what if biosystems (such as cells and microorganisms) have already invented quantum computing, actively monitoring their own internal states so that reflective consciousness of that fact and its meaning would become a peculiarly human experience? Johnjoe McFadden has conducted research and published the results relevant to this question, specifically on what he refers to as adaptive or directed mutation in such microorganisms as *E. coli* and mycobacterium tuberculosis. In a recent essay on HIV/ AIDS (Todd 2007) and in my paper "Unconscious Mental Factors in HIV Infection" (2008), I pointed out that if biosystems do process information quantum mechanically, then they would gain a marked advantage in speed and power that would be discovered by natural selection.

Such work may lead to a paradigm shift in the scientific under-standing of the very engine of evolution itself. At the very least, it implies the end of both religious fundamentalism and the doctrine of intelligent design, which creationists have regarded as a serious competitor against evolutionary theory as an explanation of the immense and magnificent variety of living forms, past and present, including Homo sapiens endowed with reflective consciousness, a late arrival on the evolutionary stage. However, as I have already noted, the demise of religious fundamentalism does not necessarily mean the abandonment of the numinous. Indeed, a more profound scientific understanding of the origins and evolution of life can illuminate such ultimate questions as the emergence of mind and consciousness as well as the existence of God. Humankind's concepts and images of God themselves need to evolve, as I shall argue on the way to uncovering the theological reality of Hans Küng (2007) that God is both greater than the world and also in it. The Jungian notion of the archetypes as timeless cosmic ordering and regulating principles serves as a depth psychological framing of such an insight.

The Universe, Active Information, and Archetypes

To approach such questions as those addressing the origins of life, the emergence of consciousness, and the existence of God, it will be necessary first to consider the information properties to be discovered in the development of matter itself, prior to the emergence of even the most primitive life forms. Paul Davies has suggested that primitive life forms may have been fast-tracked to life by some sort of quantum mechanical process or search algorithm (2004, 75). The reader will note that I have emphasized the process of discovery of active information properties in matter, albeit at a subatomic level, not the notion of some external agency or "Intelligence" somehow doing the programming. Analogously, mind and consciousness emerge in biological systems that have evolved beyond a critical threshold of complexity and self-organization. Mind and consciousness are not mysteriously beamed into such systems from some outside metaphysical source referred to as "God."

Such outmoded concepts of God are something of a soft target for skeptics partly, I believe, because they omit treating the problem of the origins and emergence of life while having practically nothing to say about a possibly nontrivial role of quantum mechanical processes (or computing) in its genesis. Such processes may be involved in evolving life from a prebiotic soup and in mutation. Strict neo-Darwinists may, of course, wish to postulate the existence of a principle analogous to natural selection as applying to the universe through backward extrapolation, so that states of matter which will eventually be fit for living organisms and consciousness somehow have an advantage. However, such a principle would be little more than a petitio principii, and if used to describe the improbable conditions in a universe that permit sentient life forms, it would simply be a restatement of the anthropic principle as described, for instance, by Penrose (2004). And naturally, as Penrose has also pointed out, in an infinite universe eventually even the most improbable contingencies will sooner or later occur without the need to invoke an external designer-God or super Programmer to explain them. The anthropic principle does not necessarily imply a universe evolving with humanity as a teleological goal. In its purely scientific formulation, this principle only states the conditions that are contingently necessary for the emergence of sentient life and consciousness. It does not address the possibility of a process (or incarnational) theology or archetypal psychology in which a numinous principle is implicit to the evolutionary process itself.

This brings the discussion back to the evolution of matter and to the notion of physicist David Bohm (2002) and his colleague Basil Hiley, who wrote "that even the quantum level can be thought to have, via active information, a primitive mindlike quality though it obviously has no consciousness" (Hiley and Pylkkänen 2005, 22). More specifically, the quantum potential appears to be "some kind of internal energy which carries information about the environment. The whole process, particle plus active environment is being formed partly from within, requiring no external force to determine its future behaviour" (ibid., 19). In this way the quantum potential differs from the classical "push-pull" potential on the level of macroscopic objects like billiard balls. Hiley reminds readers that when considering the root of the word *information*, the original meaning is that of putting form into process, and together with Bohm, he considers information to be "a link or bridge between the mental and the physical sides" of reality (ibid., 23). Thus it is possible to disentangle the notion of mind from that of consciousness which is an evolutionary emergent property in matter of such complexity and organization as that characteristic of the human brain.

This perspective, especially with its notion of a rudimentary mindlike quality associated with the quantum potential, may have implications that could demolish Dawkins's central argument. This notion is perhaps all the more shocking because it has been postulated by eminent physicists, not by theologians like Teilhard de Chardin or other scientific apostates. Wolfgang Pauli, who formulated the famous exclusion principle and collaborated with depth psychologist C. G. Jung, expressed views similar to those of Bohm. Pauli wrote of the unconscious archetypes as cosmic ordering and regulating principles responsible for the patterned information and mathematical lawfulness to be found in the physical world.

Pauli considered the archetypes to exemplify Bohr's complementarity principle, being both mental and physical in nature. The exclusion principle, as the explanation of the ordering and complexity of elements on the periodic table, needs to be understood in light of Pauli's philosophical thought as a whole, as outlined, for instance, by the late Kalervo Laurikainen (1988). I shall discuss the contributions of Pauli and Bohm in more detail in chapter 3. Suffice it to say that their epistemological position on the mind-matter relation is that of a relationship of complementarity or dual-aspect monism. In his concept of a "U-field," Pauli regarded the unconscious as the psychological counterpart of the field concept in physics and just as much a reality as matter itself. The German word Pauli used for archetypal symbols was *unanschaulich*, which translates roughly into unvisualizable, "a metaphysical reality more material than what physics and depth psychology would characterise as real" (Atmanspacher 2011, 4).

When Bohm, toward the end of his life, considered humanity to be the "mirror created by the universe to reflect upon itself" and contemplated a Mind far beyond the collective one of the species itself, he was overtly referring to a transcendent order of existence (2002, 389). Similarly, Pauli's cosmic ordering principles point to something numinous in his concept of the universe and beyond his own personal cosmic religious consciousness. However, such notions require further reasoned argument and connection with scientific facts, such as those concerning the origins of life and the possible quantum mechanical processes involved in the mutation of microorganisms and even consciousness. Could it be that a universe thus understood needs no proofs by contingency for the existence of God? Perhaps, as Shalom has argued, such a universe is "not possible without a God," given that "the existential ground of all being is commonly called God" (1989, 485). With these provocative comments, I turn now to living organisms and to what might be termed "the engine of evolution."

The Engine of Evolution

In the traditional neo-Darwinian paradigm, the figurative engine of evolution, namely, the natural selection of chance variations, functions according to purely classical laws as does the mechanism of mutation itself. The engine runs quite mechanically and nonteleologically, so that any impression of its being externally "directed" or purposive is illusory, according to the paradigm. Until late in the twentieth century, any quasi-Lamarckian notion of the adaptive (purposive) inheritance of acquired characteristics or of direction in evolution was considered to be perilously close to the teleology of creationism or intelligent design and hence pseudoscientific.

The Jesuit paleontologist Teilhard de Chardin (1964) could write of a "within of matter" and of an apparent telos in evolution, culminating in the formation of a noosphere or membrane of consciousness coexisting with the biosphere and enfolding the closed curvature of the earth. But such notions were too mystical for scientists and too scientific for the theologians of his day, such that he was silenced by the Vatican. Teilhard's vision of evolution, however, was respected by the eminent biologist Julian Huxley, who wrote the introduction to Teilhard's book *The Phenomenon of Man* and may have found some vindication in the tough-minded domain of quantum physics.

The internalist perspective, to which I alluded briefly in applying quantum mechanics to life, had not been seriously considered until the mid-late twentieth century, with the contributions, for example, of Erwin Schrödinger (1992) and McFadden and Al-Khalili, who have suggested "that the macroscopic behavior of cells and such molecules as RNA and DNA might be determined by the dynamics of individual particles and thereby be subject to quantum rather than classical laws" (1999, 209). Schrödinger held the view that quantum fluctuations produce mutations, while McFadden and Al-Khalili have provided a quantum mechanical model of what they referred to as "adaptive mutations." This formulation is a radical departure from the neo-Darwinian theory "founded on the principle that mutations occur randomly and the direction of evolutionary change is provided by selection for advantageous mutations" (ibid., 203).

A paradigm shift may therefore be occurring in the scientific understanding of the engine of evolution itself. As Davies has put it, without some process like quantum computation, "it would probably have taken longer than the entire age of the universe (about 13 billion years) for even a single protein to have formed by chance, even if all matter was made up of prebiotic soup" (2004, 76).

In *The Mind of God*, Davies seems to have been impressed enough by the nonrandomness and sheer mathematical beauty of cosmology and evolution that he wrote, "I cannot believe that our existence in this universe is a mere quirk of fate, an accident of history, an incidental blip in the great cosmic drama.... The existence of mind on some planet in the universe is surely a fact of fundamental significance. Through conscious beings the universe has generated self-awareness. This can be no trivial detail, no by-product of mindless, purposeless forces. We are truly meant to be here" (1992, 232).

However, in what follows, I shall argue that active quantum information and the Jungian archetypes as timeless cosmic ordering and regulating principles are *implicit* to the evolutionary process, which transcends humanity but in which human beings consciously participate by creating culture, including science and religion. As I have already noted, it is through the emergent consciousness of humanity that the universe reflects upon itself.

Evolution and Quantum Mechanics

The work of several eminent twentieth-century physicists could be construed as a significant catalyst of a paradigm shift whereby quantum mechanics would become integral to the theoretical explanation of evolution. Fritz-Albert Popp referred to "the chaotic and senseless goals of neo-Darwinism" in his outline of some empirical studies relevant to thinking of evolutionary phenomena in terms of quantum rather than classical laws (1989, 165). Conrad (1990) questioned why the pattern processing capabilities of cells and organisms seem to be so much greater than those achievable with present-day computers. His "self-assembly" model consisted of a hierarchical scheme of biological information processing from the quantum level to macroscopic cellular and organismic planes. He posited a form of quantum computing as an explanatory tool with respect to the mechanisms or "engine" of evolution.

Conrad rejected the classical system as inadequate to the understanding of evolution, proposing instead that such phenomena as quantum information processing and computation are necessary. In Conrad's own words, "electrons, protons, photons, and various quasi particles are on a scale size at which the quantum potential becomes relevant and to the extent that the dynamics of particles guide the docking process, self-assembly will proceed with an efficacy which cannot be understood in terms of classical analogues" (1990, 751). Self-assembly results from a quantum-facilitated search, the results of which are scaled up to the macroscopic level.

But this, as we shall presently see, is relevant to the understanding both of mutation, resulting from the "quantum fluctuations" to which Schrödinger (1992) originally referred, and of the kind of quantum search algorithm that may have fast-tracked matter to life an estimated 4 billion years ago. Even viewed from its traditional biological perspective, random mutation is to the theory of evolution what Paul Davies's purposive ideas in *The Mind of God* and in his paper, "Does Quantum Mechanics Play a Non-trivial Role in Life?" (2004), could be to the proponents of intelligent design who believe that they are proposing a serious and scientifically testable theory that can compete with evolution. Intelligent design does not satisfy Popper's falsifiability criterion of what characterizes a scientific theory.

However, quantum mechanically induced adaptive mutation would present natural selection with a much richer and more varied spectrum of choices than that caused only by environmental mutagens such as UV light and cytotoxic chemicals. In both cases, information generated at the microphysical (quantum) level is transduced upwardly to the mesoscopic (cellular or microorganism) and macroscopic levels. The underlying mathematics of these processes, as well as the active information and computational parallelism that determine them, eliminate the notions of mindless randomness and chance that have dominated thought in the neo-Darwinian paradigm of evolution for the past century. The concept of mind as active information or archetypes, on the other hand, may provide a much better fit to evolutionary data. To consider this proposition, I now turn in more detail to the contributions of Matsuno and McFadden, who are among the scientists creating the conditions for a revolution in the understanding of evolution from a classical to a quantum mechanical framework.

Biosystems and Quantum Information

Matsuno (2000), in asking whether a biology of quantum information exists, addresses some of the biomolecular systems that might exploit quantum mechanical effects. His paper on this theme argued a detailed case for the proposition that quantum-level information is being processed in biological systems. Alluding to physicist Richard Feynman's dictum that whatever humans invent, nature has arrived there first, Matsuno questioned whether biosystems had beaten humanity to the invention of quantum computing, proposing a "quantum mechanical model underlying a neuronal synaptic transmitter release based on a tunnelling process" (2000, 41). He then turned to the issue of measurement and, in adopting an internalist ecological perspective, proposed that a sequence of measurements proceeding internally generates information.

Biological computations founded on internal measurement provide an irreversible enhancement of organization and quantum coherence. "Once it is accepted," Matsuno argued, "that biological information processing has a quantum mechanical underpinning, two further concepts become important. Quantum coherence through exchange interaction and then the enhancement of this through quantum entanglement" (2000, 43).

According to Matsuno, quantum information in biology focuses upon the capacity of molecules to approach global coordination from within. In now turning to the work of McFadden on adaptive mutation, the move from an implicit or unconscious investment in the externalist classical framework of evolutionary theory to the internalist quantum mechanical framework will be more fully explicated.

As I have already implied, this is a shift from understanding evolution (including that of life and mind) in classical terms to understanding it in terms of the quantum laws that govern the internal and microscopic level of matter. Some readers might construe this perspective as being in a direct line of conceptual descent from thinkers like Teilhard de Chardin, for whom such developments in physics as those of quantum information theory and computing were not available. And yet much of the critique provided by proponents of neo-Darwinism seems to be stuck in a classical scientific framework of explanation, as though the quantum revolution had never occurred. So much so that, as Davies has put it, the "classical chance hypothesis" of the origins of life seems unsatisfactory. And I would add, the rule of chance may turn out to be itself a matter of secular religious faith!

Furthermore, conceptualizing the genetic code as a quantum code permits a vastly enhanced computational speed made possible through multiple superpositions, so that greater numbers of errors in base-pairing and hence mutations could occur. Acting as biological quantum computers, biosystems, including cells and microorganisms, would be able to search multiple mutational states simultaneously, allowing for the selection of adaptive as well as random mutations, as McFadden and Al-Khalili (1999) have suggested. McFadden drew my attention to a paper by himself and colleagues on mutation in multiple drug-resistant strains of *Mycobacterium tuberculosis* (Ghanekar, et al. 1999). Their empirical work on this particular microorganism had provided what he described as "hints of the adaptive mutation phenomenon," although further work was required to more convincingly "nail it to quantum mechanical effects" (personal communication, 2007).

The truly revolutionary ideas in the publications of Matsuno and McFadden and his colleagues are those involving living cells acting as quantum measuring devices able to assess quantum processes occurring internally and the shift from a classical to a quantum explanation of such phenomena as mutation that may be adaptive rather than random in nature. Perhaps the greatest conceptual leap beyond the confines of neo-Darwinism is the notion that there may be much more to mutation than chance errors in DNA or RNA bases, resulting from either quantum mechanical processes or the external environment. More needs to be said, however, about the phenomenon of directed mutation and the implied challenge to traditional neo-Darwinian evolutionary theory.

Natural Selection of Nonrandom Variations

McFadden and Al-Khalili have pointed out that the principle that mutations occur randomly with respect to the direction of evolutionary change has been challenged by the phenomenon they have termed "adaptive mutations." Arguing that no satisfactory theory exists to account for how a cell can selectively mutate certain genes in response to environmental signals, they noted that spontaneous mutations are initiated by quantum events such as the shift of a single proton from one site to an adjacent one (1999, 204). This is essentially the "quantum jump" effect described by Schrödinger. McFadden and Al-Khalili considered the wave function describing the quantum state of the genome as being in a coherent linear superposition of states describing "shifted and unshifted protons." Accelerated rates of decoherence, they argued, may significantly increase the rate of production of the mutated state.

Referring to the Copenhagen interpretation of quantum mechanics formulated by Bohr, Heisenberg, Pauli, and others concerning the role of the observer, McFadden and Al-Khalili (1999, 205) make the provocative claim that living cells (like conscious observers) can themselves form unique quantum measuring devices that monitor and probe quantum processes occurring internally. They sum up their notion of the cell acting as a quantum computer, as they put it, able to "sample the vast mutational spectra and to collapse towards those that provide the greatest advantage" (ibid., 211). The phenomenon of adaptive mutation, demonstrated with *E. coli*, seems likely to be implicated in the development of multiple drug-resistant strains of *Mycobacterium tuberculosis* and perhaps HIV in response to environments created by antiretroviral drugs.

The conclusions drawn by McFadden and Al-Khalili may have profound implications for understanding the role of active information associated with the quantum potential for a theory of evolution which, far from being constrained solely by randomness and chance and the externalist perspective of classical physics, is illuminated by an internalist and quantum mechanical framework. Mutation thus conceived is not solely a random or chance matter but adaptive or directed in a manner that is compatible with quantum mechanics and information theory. However, this astonishing argument needs further elaboration, if only because it means the beginning of the end of a purely classical understanding of matter, particularly once matter has evolved into entities both animate and conscious.

What would become of Dawkins's God delusion if in fact life and such phenomena as mutation are inconveniently determined by quantum mechanics rather than classical laws? McFadden and Al-Khalili's conclusions, as well as those of Conrad (1990), Matsuno (2000), Davies (2004), and Penrose (1999, 2004), will probably lead to a paradigm shift in evolutionary theory that incorporates some distinctly Lamarckian (purposive) mechanisms, especially if further experimental data confirm the significance of such phenomena as adaptive or directed mutation. Dawkin's dogmatic and rigid form of neo-Darwinism would collapse.

Dawkins's Crunch: Quantum Information

The inevitable "crunch" for Dawkins's argument comes with the recognition that all biological phenomena involve the movement of fundamental particles such as protons and electrons within living cells and informational molecules such as RNA and DNA. (The term *crunch* is a metaphor from cosmology concerning the end of a process of contraction of the universe, reversing the expansion phase that has continued since the Big Bang.) As such, and as McFadden and physicists as far back as Schrödinger have known, movements of fundamental particles are best described by quantum rather than classical mechanics. Quantum phenomena occur in biological systems, although the implications have yet to be fully explored especially in the understanding of such deadly microbes as TB and HIV, which represent globally salient evolutionary challenges for Homo sapiens.

These considerations, of course, have profound significance for attempts to illuminate the origins of life and other big-picture questions such as the emergence of mind and consciousness whereby evolution becomes both cultural and directed. I shall have much more to say about these ultimate questions and the implications for theology in subsequent chapters. However, the race to produce a viable quantum computer (by humans) is motivated in part at least by the spiritual quest to comprehend the evolutionary origins of life as well as the destiny of humankind. The information thus created will have an almost ineffable epistemological significance for humanity while contributing to a theology of the third millennium inspired by the same fire that breathes life into the equations of science. If as Hiley and Pylkkänen (2005) and others have suggested, even the quantum level can be thought to have via active information, a primitive mindlike quality, and if indeed nature has already invented quantum computing as an evolutionary tool, then the old classical view of the world is dead.

Furthermore, mind, rather than being somehow miraculously added to the evolution of the universe, would be as intrinsic to it as Bohm's implicate order or Pauli's archetypal cosmic ordering and regulating principles. This sentiment, expressed sublimely in Bohm's idea that humanity is the mirror reflecting the universe to itself, may represent a metaphorical crunch for Dawkins's God Delusion, in which neo-Darwinism is more of a doctrine about nature rather than an empirical explanation of it, and for the absurdity of the intelligent design argument.

Why Active Information Is Not Intelligent Design

I have discussed the difference between genetic and quantum information in reference to the mystery of the origins of life, mutation, and biological complexity in the evolution of living organisms. As Davies, for instance, has pointed out, quantum superposition and entanglement permit computational parallelism, so that the enhancement becomes exponential, implying an enormous increase in computational speed and power compared to classical information processing (2004, 70). Similarly, neuroscientist Karl Pribram in reassessing consciousness draws attention to the notion that in shifting from classic "bits" to "bytes" in thinking about information processing, "meaning resides in the complexity of the pattern rather than in the arrangement of simple elements" (2004, 15). Jungian archetypes are reflected in mathematical regularities and instinctual patterns.

Neither quantum computing nor the decryption of meaning from complex patterns of information imply the existence of an external "intelligent" designer or God responsible for such phenomena. According to the anthropic principle, it is sufficient that the conditions of the universe are such that these phenomena are possible. Active information and even the recognition of meaning in complex patterns do not necessarily entail intelligent design of the universe by an external creator God. The evolution of life and such processes as those of cellular repair and differentiation as well as the elimination of foreign pathogens such as microbes by the immune system involve complex pattern recognition, although the spiritual search for meaning seems to be a uniquely human attribute. Human beings draw upon the informational structures that comprise culture and science in the programming of their brains. And reflectively conscious human beings use suitably programmed brains to evolve culture.

I now wish to make a sharper distinction between active information patterns and structures as well as the quantum computing and the pseudoscientific doctrine of intelligent design, which may bear a superficial resemblance to it. Intelligent design is the thesis that skeptics such as Dawkins have rightly debunked as unscientific because it is unfalsifiable. The intelligent design argument, proposed by creationists and others as a scientific competitor to Darwin's theory of evolution, invokes the existence of a hyperintelligent and omniscient designer of the universe, one responsible for the increasing states of complexity, order, and central organization discernible in the evolution of matter culminating in the creation of human beings. The designer-God is supposed to have kick-started life once matter reached the level of complexity preprogramed into it and then to have intervened again to create Homo sapiens in His own image. However, perhaps it will facilitate clear exposition if we dissect the intelligent design argument into its components and discuss it in more detail.

According to most versions of this argument, such highly improbable coincidences as the values of six cosmic constants necessary to sustain life are explained, together with the development of sentient beings, as being due to the miraculous intervention of a divine being. Such an explanation is a grotesque distortion of the valid scientific anthropic principle by adopting the teleological notion that the universe was designed with humanity in the mind of God as a predetermined goal from the very beginning. Penrose (2004) rejects this strong version of the anthropic principle with its implicit teleological anticipation of the evolutionary ascent of humanity. He thinks that this version places too much weight on the shoulders of the creator, whose existence would be necessary if one asks who (or what) presumably held the appearance of humanity in mind in the beginning.

According to intelligent design, the existence of consciousness and of the human soul, somehow beamed into the fertilized egg at conception, are likewise attributed to an external supernatural agency. Not only does God have to sustain the entire universe in being, he is not spared the tiresome work of creating as many separate souls as human beings are conceived per unit in time. At present this figure is more than six billion and counting, even if one forgets those who have ever inhabited planet Earth.

Dawkins has alluded to design in the universe as an "illusion" explicable in terms of natural selection, a position with which I thoroughly agree as a parsimonious and empirically testable form of explanation. Intelligent design is not characterized by these essential qualities, and when stripped of its pseudoscientific linguistic mask, the argument is little more than a modern creation myth. In this genesis myth, God is not given the dignity of being a mathematical genius or even computer literate, let alone given the status of a super programmer in a universe conceived as a kind of Turing machine or information processing device. Moreover, as Dawkins has pointed out with respect to the accumulation of improbable events that are used to argue a case for the existence of a designer God, this argument renders such a concept of God improbable in the extreme. In the manner of infinite regress, the cause of multiple events, themselves improbable, is itself necessarily highly improbable.

In fact, intelligence and mind construed as active information are precisely what the so-called intelligent design argument for the existence of God lacks. Intelligent design may recognize the existence of complex systems, but it misses the crucial element of biological complexity understood as information-based. For instance, the intelligent design concept of the eye as a complex organ, so apparently perfect in its function, passes over the informational complexity of its gradual evolution completely. Instead of trying to understand the origins of life as a problem into which quantum computers and information theory may provide enlightenment, intelligent design assumes that all that is required is the intelligence of the designer, not the active and patterned information to be discovered in matter itself. Often, as the history of science attests, discoveries awaken aesthetic rapture due to the elegance and beauty of the mathematical insights and empirical laws described, for instance, by Penrose as characterizing the lawfulness and structure of the universe. Penrose wrote, "a beautiful idea has a much better chance of being correct than an ugly one" (1999, 544).

Worse still perhaps, the intelligence imputed to the designer is inferred by mere analogy from such apparently well-designed organs as the eye if not also from the clockwork universe of Newton. However, neither the functioning of the eye nor Newton's laws require a creator or lawmaker, a scandal for religious fundamentalists who confuse mathematical and empirical laws with the laws of governance used in courts. Scientific understanding of how life emerged from a prebiotic soup and of the properties of active information immanent in prelife matter do not necessarily require the existence of an external intelligent designer-God.

Such a designer, like Yahweh at the beginning of the Old Testament, broods over a primordial chaos or void like that portrayed in the various scriptural creation stories, including Genesis. The negentropy (negative entropy) upon which life feeds according to Schrödinger (1992) and the emergence of mind and reflective consciousness do not require an anthropomorphic God or proofs by contingency of His existence. (As Schrödinger intended it, the term *negative entropy* represented entropy, as he put it, with a negative sign [1992, 73]. Thus it refers to the ever-increasing states of order, complexity, and central or self-organization that characterize living animate matter.)

The Vacuous Meme Hypothesis

These considerations lead me to consider the meme hypothesis of the origins of religious systems of thought, argued, for instance, by Dawkins and his colleague Susan Blackmore. I include it here because the transmission of memes as patterns of information, either by imitation or in such a way as to be stored in memory, is integral to the explanation of the apparent persistence and evolutionary success of religious ideas. I shall attempt to show that the hypothesis is vacuous, having no substantive connection with either the notion of archetypes as cosmic ordering principles or active information at the quantum level as an alternative explanatory framework.

For Dawkins and Blackmore, the meme is the cultural analogue of the gene in biological evolution, and complexes of them are selected because they allegedly have survival value for competing sociocultural groups in human populations. Religions are examples of so-called memeplexes (or meme complexes) whose function is to provide believers with paradigms through which philosophical and even cosmological questions are resolved, usually with the certainty of proclaimed articles of faith and irrespective of whether such answers are compatible with empirical science.

According to Dawkins, religious memes have survival value in the meme pool because of their supposed "merit" (2006, 199) in providing reassurance of survival after death, the status of moral superiority, and virtue and protection of the host from hostile meme intrusions or paradigms of thought, including those of other religions and of scientific philosophy. Heroic self-sacrifice and virtue, even that of martyrdom, is by group consensus rewarded with instant paradise at death or the immortality of canonization to sainthood, posthumously. Conversion of nonbelievers or infidels is designed to propagate the memetic system as well as providing the surety of eternal bliss, while the codification of the memes in sacred scriptures ensures the survival of memeplexes over time, sometimes for millennia.

Thus expressed, the meme hypothesis may seem to be both seductively attractive and unassailable to criticism by rationalist minds, partly because it is very intelligently cast as scientific in its formulation, even in the more elaborate versions published by Dawkins and Blackmore. The sheer creativity of the memetic explanation for religion deserves to be read in its original sources the way certain contributions to the history of ideas should be studied as instructive examples of error.

However, I argue that the meme hypothesis is vacuous and unenlightening regarding those concepts of mind and of the numinous that have emerged from the integration of quantum physics and depth psychology as well as neuroscience. Memetics is brought in to do heavy explanatory lifting, while ultimately dropping the weight of necessary substantive argument.

Viewed as patterns of information or units of cultural transmission, there is little to distinguish religious meme complexes in structure or mode of communication from those of mathematics and other purely secular scientific disciplines or philosophies. All are ostensibly addressed to the peculiarly human need to find meaning in the origins of our own species as well as those of the universe itself. Science has its own ethical and moral canons and the promise of such rapturously anticipated rewards as Nobel Prizes as well as the immortality of publication in prestigious journals.

Beautiful music and art could be construed as self-replicating memeplexes (analogous to RNA or DNA), perpetuating religious ideas, as Dawkins suggests (2006, 199). But logically, this notion is not particularly illuminating with respect to the rapture evoked by medieval or Baroque masterpieces in those who may never have been indoctrinated with theological beliefs or with regard to similar states evoked by the mathematically ordered works of Tallis, Bach, Mozart, or, for that matter, Gershwin. I have known scientific agnostics who use such works as the Magnificat of J. S. Bach to facilitate their creativity in mathematics or to enhance their focus in writing complex papers for publication. The feelings of awe elicited by a great cathedral are not reducible to knowledge of the engineering that built it nor is the theology encoded in it explained by the blocks of stone used to construct it. As Schrödinger was well aware, mystical experience and the sense of the numinous are not contingent upon the religious and traditional theological memeplexes to which Dawkins refers.

Another perhaps fatal flaw in the meme hypothesis is the difficulty in agreeing upon a definition of memetics, a difficulty conceded by Blackmore in her book *The Meme Machine*. The vacuousness of the hypothesis as an explanation of all religious phenomena is due in part at least to this confusion, compounding the problems to which I have already referred. Memes simply cannot obtain the status of genes with such scandalous imprecision of scientific definition, in spite of the illusions of rigor and quantization created by the use of concepts borrowed from neo-Darwinism and genetics such as pool, diversity, selection and survival value.

Such vagueness is concealed beneath the apparent sophistication of Dawkins's demolition of religion, while leaving the door open to the danger that the term *meme* will be used as a *petitio principii* or explanation of itself, as occurs in such tautological explanations as "heat burns because it has a fiery quality" or "living organisms exist because they are endowed with vital attributes." However, I would be surprised if Dawkins intended to regress to explanations of religion in terms of the essences and vital forces (entelechies) that characterized pre-Copernican theological argument as well as some domains of science prior to the nineteenth century, for instance, the phlogiston theory in chemistry and pre-Mendelian accounts of the origins of life.

The Scandal of Sexuality and Lost Wholeness

No attempt to counter religious fundamentalism would be complete without engaging the scandal of human sexuality—not only the recent scandals involving clergy, which have shaken the foundations of Christendom, but also the chronic inability of evangelical and conservative theology to integrate the sexual dimension into an image of human wholeness instead of perpetuating the splitting of the bodily and numinous aspects of full humanness. I shall begin my account of this malaise and of the need for a restoration of lost innocence and wholeness to both theology and humanity, with a story.

Among the many tales told about Michelangelo's painting of the frescoes on the ceiling of the Sistine Chapel in Rome is one in which the artist is admonished by a cardinal for the nudity depicted, for instance, in his representation of the primordial Adam in full view, incidentally, of the Creator God of Genesis whose extended hand almost touches that of his son. The artist was advised to cover the offending genitalia in spite of the counsel from God, recorded in the Genesis myth, to increase and multiply and in spite of the fact that before succumbing to the temptation of the serpent, Adam and Eve were supposed to have existed in a state of original innocence, devoid of shame about their organs of increase or the earth from which Adam, as the symbol of humankind, had been fashioned. Fortunately for future generations of human beings as well as for the integrity of the frescoes, Michelangelo followed his inspiration and disobeyed the cardinal, leaving Adam in his pristine state. The artist's revenge, however, was both priceless and timeless. He painted the cardinal into the hellish scene of the last judgment depicted on the rear wall behind the high altar in the chapel, where he continues to stare out at pilgrims and visitors to this day.

Reconciling the apparent opposites of matter and spirit, sexuality and numinosity, remains a formidable challenge for theology. And yet, in Catholic and Orthodox Christianity, at least, the doctrine of the incarnation of God in Christ implies the reconciliation and union of opposites into a state not of opposition but of wholeness, as C. G. Jung, for instance, noted in his extensive writings on comparative religion. If there is a complementarity between matter and spirit, neither need be denied or renounced; to do so results in the malaise, manifested recently in the abhorrent sexual scandals involving the clergy.

No need exists to repeat here the endless arguments, many of them from theologians themselves, for a realignment of religious doctrine with scientific understanding of human sexuality. I canvassed such arguments in my book *AIDS: A Pilgrimage to Healing* (1992). There is a need, however, to discuss the obstacles created by conservative and fundamentalist religious dogmas to the creation of bridges between science and religion and for the integration of sexuality with personality and spirituality necessary for being fully human. Perhaps ecclesiastical institutions need to take incarnational theology more seriously, rather than promoting doctrines that imply an imbalance between spirit and matter while maintaining a childish literalism in the interpretation of scriptures, as did the cardinal in the story about Michelangelo's frescoes in which Adam and God have an apparently equal stature. Similarly, neither the embodiment nor the divinity of God in Christ or in humanity itself need be denied.

In the early centuries of Christianity, as Jung has pointed out, the church may have encouraged the sublimation of sexual instincts to counter the depravity known in ancient Rome. Such sublimation may even have been necessary for the advancement of culture and civilization as well as the rise of Christianity. However, repression is not the same as sublimation, resulting in instincts being driven into opposition in the unconscious, returning in the unwanted form of compulsions and neuroses or in such scandals as those that have been exposed in the clergy.

Insisting that all sexuality must be subservient to the exclusive end of procreation according to a so-called natural order rooted in biblical literalism has resulted in some quite unnatural notions that, if followed to their logical conclusions, would mean a cruel prohibition of heterosexual acts after menopause in women or subsequent to hysterectomy as well as a condemnation of birth control, which may be vital to the survival of humanity. The definition of homosexuality as an objective disorder is not only contrary to scientific consensus, it has stigmatized countless human beings, including such benefactors as Michelangelo, Isaac Newton, and mathematician Alan Turing while contributing to behavior patterns that put people at risk for HIV infection. Splitting between sexuality and spirituality is conducive neither to mental health nor integration and personal wholeness, as I argued in *AIDS: A Pilgrimage to Healing* (1992).

The scandal of human sexuality is, I believe, a direct consequence of confusing scripture with history and of a biblical literalism that tends to strip theology of a rich vein of archetypal myth and symbol of potential transformative significance for humankind. It also means that the idea of the incarnation of God in humanity, represented in the mythology and symbolism of Christ, is maintained at a level of infantile concretism rather than being grasped firmly as a mirroring of the destiny of humankind to complete the evolution of God. This understanding of incarnational theology, however, would entail a total transformation in the myth of Genesis (which I address in chapter 6).

The New Genesis: Lamarckian Anomalies

Scientific enlightenment into the origins of life, perhaps with quantum mechanics playing the nontrivial role discussed by Davies, promises to provide a new genesis in which even the neo-Darwinian theory of evolution is transformed. Again, quantum laws would replace classical ones in a new paradigm of explanation encompassing microscopic through to macroscopic phenomena as exemplified in the contributions of such thinkers as Matsuno, McFadden and Al-Khalili. That life may have emerged in the evolving chaos of the RNA world, as Steele (1998), for example, has suggested, and come into being through quantum mechanical processes may be a more exciting as well as scientifically valid story of genesis than any biblical account written thousands of years ago by humankind in its animistic infancy.

According to the traditional neo-Darwinian paradigm, the doctrine of the natural selection of chance variations still prevails in spite of empirical evidence for such anomalies as directed or adaptive mutation in microorganisms (McFadden and Al-Khalili 1999) and aspects of culture not clearly relevant to mere survival that are incommensurable with the theory. In the words of McFadden and Al-Khalili, "living cells could act as biological quantum computers able to simultaneously explore multiple mutational states (in superposition) and collapse towards those that provide the greatest advantage" (ibid., 210). Concepts such as that of adaptive mutation have the signature of Lamarck written all over them, as Ross Honeywill has argued in his book *Lamarck's Evolution: Two Centuries of Genius and Jealousy* (2008), as does experimental demonstration of the inheritance of acquired immunity in the form of antibody diversity passed through the germline from one generation to the next. Specifically, immunologist Ted Steele argues that such Lamarckian mechanisms as, "reverse transcription and soma-to-germline feedback processes.... allow directional fine-tuning of immunity over evolutionary time" (2009, 438, 444). This means penetrating the Weismann barrier, which was one of the conceptual pillars of neo-Darwinism. The Weismann barrier had precluded soma-to-germline transmission of genetic information. In HIV infection the retrovirus transforms CD4+T cells into destructive narcissistic clones of itself through reverse transcription in a form of Trojan horse strategy so that HIV is no longer recognized as a not-self pathogen and therefore eliminated. Reverse transcription is simply copying an RNA template into DNA, and in the case of HIV the retrovirus thus becomes integrated into the CD4+T cell, a vital component of cellular immune defense (Steele 1998, 51). Steele has turned the Weismann barrier to a soma-to-germline transmission of genetic information into a fiction while demonstrating nonrandom or directed mutation. In cultural evolution, concepts of transpersonal meaning and purpose would be compatible with scientific discoveries such as these and with Teilhard de Chardin's vision of a noosphere or envelope of meaning and consciousness surrounding the curvature of the earth. Teilhard's vision of a noosphere implies embracing a geopolitical holism in which humanity collectively becomes responsible for challenges such as global warming that threaten the ecosystems upon which all life and all interconnected human beings depend. (See Todd 2008 and 2011 for an extension of this argument.)

Pauli thought that synchronicity phenomena may have characterized the beginnings of life, perhaps because this concept implies an archetypal event involving meaningful though acausal connection instead of senseless chaos. However, such scientifically dubious hypothesizing is unnecessary in an era in which quantum information theory seems to have such promising applications so that the origins of life may not need to be hidden as if beneath a veil.

Davies views the origin of life as a type of search problem, the puzzle being how a figurative soup of classical molecular building blocks could discover such an extremely improbable combination as would yield a simple life form in a reasonable period of time. As it would take longer than the age of the universe (13 billion years) for even a single protein to form by chance, Davies argues, the classical chance hypothesis seems unsatisfactory; and, of course, no random variations would have emerged as yet, to be naturally selected according to neo-Darwinian mechanisms. Darwin, incidentally, had no idea of how life started, and quantum mechanics and information theories, as well as their possible role as the "spark," were twentieth-century developments.

A radical alternative to the barren chance hypothesis is quantum mechanics. As quantum systems can exist in superpositions of states, they may search out a vast array of alternatives simultaneously. Can quantum mechanics explain how matter was fast-tracked to life by discovering biologically potent molecular configurations much faster than using classical estimates? As Davies has suggested, this is the motivation behind the quest for a quantum computer that would have what Feynman refers to as its computational parallelism. In particular, quantum superposition and entanglement represent a type of such computational parallelism that results in a prodigious increase in computational speed and power in comparison to classical information processing.

Thus, as I have indicated with some experimental examples, if biological systems can process information quantum mechanically, they would gain a distinct, exponential advantage in speed and power that would be discovered by natural selection and amplified (as appears to be happening with such microbes as HIV in relation to humans) in terms of competitive advantage.

The new biogenesis seems likely to depend upon advances in quantum information theory, with the genetic code regarded as or even replaced by a quantum code (as the work of McFadden and Al-Khalili has suggested). Such advances in turn, could result in a paradigm shift in understanding one of science's greatest mysteries, namely, the origins of life. However, a vexed question now presents itself. If nature has already invented quantum computing and if, as Hiley has suggested, mind as active information though devoid of consciousness exists even at the quantum level, how is artificial intelligence to be understood in devices created by humans? And what is to be made of the nonalgorithmic and noncomputable aspects of intelligence such as mathematical insights and creative inspiration in science and music with which Penrose, for instance, is concerned? Penrose writes, "If we can see that the role of consciousness is nonalgorithmic when forming mathematical judgments.... such a nonalgorithmic ingredient could be crucial in more general, nonmathematical circumstances" (1999, 535). Penrose remarks that "Dirac is unabashed in his claim that it was his keen sense of beauty that enabled him to divine his equation for the electron (the Dirac equation) while others searched in vain" (ibid., 545).

Perhaps a much broader concept of intelligence than has hitherto been considered in science needs to be contemplated, one which encompasses consciousness yet goes beyond it and whose imprint seems to exist throughout nature from the quantum level through to humanity and beyond, as Bohm and Pauli using different language have suggested. This intelligence, via quantum mechanics and computing, may be responsible for the origins of life. If so, one face of the numinous may be presenting itself to us. In evolutionary terms, this means that humanity is collectively responsible for directing the future of evolution both of the biosphere and of the noosphere. McFadden's quantum mechanical model of adaptive or directed mutation suggests how such apparent direction might work with unconscious microbes. Humans, however, are reflectively conscious, as Pauli put it, creating nature, not just evolved nature.

CHAPTER 3

Mind and Directed Evolution

To strict neo-Darwinians, including Richard Dawkins, the very idea that evolution might involve the natural selection of anything but purely random variations would be considered both pseudoscientific and "heretical." Likewise, the notion of direction in the ontogeny of matter prior to life would be vehemently suspected of heretical teleology as would the suggestion that, in and through humanity, evolution has somehow become both conscious of itself and directed. Biological skeptics like Dawkins might well argue that ideas of adaptive or directed evolution are as illusory as the appearance of design in nature used to buttress the intelligent design doctrine. However, if by making a discovery of unparalleled significance, that of the extrabiological or cultural transmission of information, human beings are able to influence not only the human genome but also the future of the biosphere as well as the noosphere, then it is difficult to doubt the existence of directed evolution once the ascent of humankind had begun.

Consider the contemporary and salient challenges to the survival of humanity on earth, the collective response to which reveals human beings as not merely passively reacting and adapting but reflectively acting upon nature. In the new genesis to which I referred in the last chapter, human beings might well have been products of natural selection, gaining an adaptive advantage over their prehominid ancestors and eventually surviving them. Now, however, human choices—selections—not memetics imitating genetics in a manner as mysterious and as inaccessible to science as the concept of God that Dawkins so zealously debunks, will probably determine our species survival.

Among the challenges to human survival, let us consider first Al Gore's inconvenient truth of global warming. In spite of the denials and arguments of passionate skeptics and pre-Copernican obscurantists, the consensus of science is that global warming is being caused largely by humankind's collective consumption and burning of fossil fuels, such as coal and oil, resulting in greenhouse gas emissions. Pure economic and political expediency and a refusal to acknowledge the consequences of such myopic consumerism for future generations, especially in the developed world, continue to exacerbate this situation. The current token containment policies in Australia and the United States have been foolishly designed to minimize the inconvenience to multinational corporations producing fossil fuels and internal combustion engines while neglecting the imperative to develop alternative technologies. Both global warming and solutions to it are contingent upon collective and conscious human choices. Only our phylogenetic evolutionary legacy manifest in aggressive consumerism and exploitation of the earth's resources for the short-term benefit of the few at the expense of the many could result in collective refusal to acknowledge and respond to the dangers posed by climate change. There is nothing random or chance-like about the corporate, nationalistic, and economic self-interest expressed in the neglect of solutions to global warming.

Nor is there anything random about the disgraceful neglect on an international scale of what I have referred to elsewhere as the "holocaust" of HIV/AIDS, another challenge to human survival (Todd 2007). HIV is a retroviral messenger with a summons to humankind to unite in combating a global microbial terrorist exhibiting awesome destructive power and constituting a grave threat to both economic and national security, especially in the developing world. The belief that primary prevention and control are a sufficient solution rests upon a social engineering model of disease while neglecting the insight expressed, for instance, by Oxford physicist Roger Penrose that overcoming the terrors of disease has often resulted from fundamental understandings in other fields such as physics (2004, 1043). In fact, the fantasy that control of HIV is economically and politically preferable to the quest for a deeper scientific understanding or even a revolution in medical science represents a form of wishful denial as well as ignoring such realities as the profit motives of pharmaceutical companies.

Responding to the global challenges of HIV/AIDS and tuberculosis will entail collective decisions to prioritize funding for innovative research and treatment initiatives. If the mutation of HIV is something other than a purely random event, then the global response of humankind will need to be highly directed and proactive while demanding the best efforts of the most advanced scientific minds. It is not the case that there is no meaning to be found in such pandemics. The meaning implicit in these phenomena is that humankind must respond to the summons that HIV-related morbidity and projected mortality rates, as well as the rates for tuberculosis, already represents for the species. When HIV is perceived as a salient threat to the developed world (as avian influenza and SARS have been), the meaning will be clear even to skeptics and those in denial.

In cultural evolutionary terms, the meaning to be found is the need for a shift in humankind's collective consciousness. This shift involves recognition of a metaphorical quantum entanglement between the developed and developing worlds with a geopolitical holism that transcends the confines of nationalism and economic self-interest, as I argued in my essay "The Neglected Holocaust" (2007). Responding to challenges to species survival such as global warming and pandemics will, I believe, entail a restored sense of the sacredness of life and of the earth itself. Restoration of lost numinosity may be facilitated by creating bridges between science and the religious traditions of East and West.

What seems to be missing in the metaphysical materialism of the West and in such notions as Dawkins's that God is a delusion is a conceptualization of God within an evolutionary framework of mind, and especially of the unconscious psyche as understood in depth psychology and in quantum physics and neuroscience. In this evolutionary framework consciousness and culture program the brain to evolve science, culture, and religion, and mind is present in rudimentary form even at the level of quantum particles (Bohm 2002, 386). Popper and Eccles (1983) refer to "three worlds" of brain, culture, and mind which are indispensable for the achievement of consciousness. The three worlds interact in a feedback loop so that consciousness or mind programs the brain to evolve culture which in turn stimulates mental development. This is familiar from the published work of such thinkers as Julian Huxley, Roger Penrose, and Teilhard de Chardin as the notion of providing direction to the evolution of culture, science, and Teilhard's noosphere. Penrose refers to three worlds—Platonic-mathematical, physical, and mental—where each "has its own reality and where each is deeply and mysteriously founded in the one that precedes it... I like to think that the Platonic world may be the most primitive of the three" (2004, 1029). It is to the role of mind in its conscious and unconscious aspects that I shall now turn in discussing manifestations of the numinous.

Unconscious Manifestations of the Numinous

Dawkins's grasp of psychology and of the mind in its conscious and unconscious aspects, by his own admission, is that of an amateur and quite rudimentary, as is revealed in his discussion of quantum mechanics and his dismissal of the Copenhagen interpretation in which the personal equation or consciousness of the observer is a prominent feature in quantum experiments. His attempt to parody the Copenhagen interpretation is incompatible with the views of such physicists as Niels Bohr, Werner Heisenberg, and Wolfgang Pauli, who were among those who first formulated it. Of contemporary physicists, Penrose takes the Copenhagen interpretation seriously while incorporating a Platonic realm of ideas and mathematical truth in his consideration of the mental and of the role of quantum physics in consciousness.

Penrose's system of thought is in certain respects similar to that of Jung and Pauli, on the one hand, with their notion of the archetypes as cosmic regulating principles and David Bohm's concept of the implicate order on the other hand. Schrödinger's (1992) treatment of mind was anything but amateurish or reductionist as the whole edifice of science rested upon constructions of the mental.

The concept of reason, subject to near apotheosis by Dawkins, is a relatively recent development in the history of ideas. It was during the French Revolution in the eighteenth century that the goddess of Reason was enthroned on the altar of Notre Dame Cathedral in Paris, supposedly to dispel the superstitions that had hitherto characterized pre-Enlightenment Catholicism. Needless to say perhaps, it was not reason that characterized the excesses of the French or the subsequent violent revolutions. Shadow qualities, including fantasies of omnipotence, are required to be successful in killing off God. Traces of this theme seem to me to exist in Freud's myth about the ancestral guilt induced in sons due to the crime of murdering a primal father as one of the origins of religion. It is probable that Freud never resolved his death wish toward his own father (projected onto Jung) and that his views on religion were never liberated from it either.

When Freud annihilated God, his zeal was invested in his system of psychoanalysis and in the project to liberate humanity from the illusion of religion. Paradoxically perhaps, Freud, while speculating about a racial unconscious as an archaic heritage of humankind's phylogenetic past manifest in dreams and cultural traditions, remained a rationalist in his conscious attitude. Jung and many of Freud's successors would subsequently adopt a more empirical approach to the numinous or God archetype. This dimension of experience had its origins both in the personal unconscious acquired during the individual's lifetime and in the collective unconscious with its mental representations of the whole history of evolution. Jung's collective unconscious and Freud's racial unconscious were somewhat overlapping concepts, though there are places in Jung's writings (for example, in *Memories, Dreams, Reflections* [1961]) where he extends the unconscious to encompass the cosmos itself.

While avoiding conflation of Freud's and Jung's formulations with those of theology, later analysts of both schools contributed to the psychological understanding of religious experience, using terms such as the unconscious God representation, image, or archetype manifest in ego consciousness. Such manifestations were of a psychic or symbolic reality or fact existing beyond ego consciousness and were not confined to the categories of space and time but rather to some unconscious primordial or timeless dimension, referred to by neuroscientist Karl Pribram (2004) as "prespacetime" and by mathematician Hans Primas (2003) as the timeless primordial reality of an *unus mundus* or one world.

Jung himself, in his essay "Psychology and Religion" remarked that "for a certain type of intellectual mediocrity characterized by enlightened rationalism, a scientific theory that simplifies matters, is a very good defense because of the tremendous faith modern man has in anything that bears the label scientific" (1940, 45). While referring to "atheism as a stupid error" (ibid., 82), Jung consistently referred to God as a "psychic fact" and tried to avoid making metaphysical assertions which he regarded as the proper domain of theology. In contributions such as his essay "Transformation Symbolism in the Mass" (1954), Jung's profound respect for theology is as evident as is his own effort to remain scrupulously empirical and scientific. Jung himself rejected the tendency to reduce theology to depth psychology (psychologism) expressed in "nothing but" types of statements, for instance, in "Transformation Symbolism in the Mass" and *Aion* (1951). In contrast, Jungian analyst Michael Fordham preferred the view "that the study of humanity must reveal the nature of God as far as it can be understood by human beings" (1985, 184). According to Jung, depth psychology could illuminate theology and facilitate the restoration of meaning to religious symbols without succumbing to the temptation to engage in dogmatic formulations.

Once one has disposed of certain archaic, infantile ideas or representations of God (which is easy for writers like Dawkins to do), one is still left with the undeniable reality of numinous experience, expressions of which include the so-called God archetype or image and such epiphanies as those of mathematical and scientific insight or illumination. These experiences are anything but illusory or delusional and are often accompanied by mystical feelings of the most rapturous and radiant beauty. Jung regarded religious experience as a priceless treasure for those who possess it (1940, 1948, 1954). Jung referred to the mass as a transformational rite corresponding to the individuation process (1954, 273).

Perhaps the most sublime epiphany of all, however, is that of the supernatural aspect of humanity revealed in the incarnation, the notion of God becoming human as represented in the historic and symbolic Christ. Jungian analyst Michael Fordham (1985), commenting upon this supernaturalness, seems to be more comfortable with a psychological perspective than a theological one. However, this may be due partly to the tendency of many theologians to think of God as remote and transcendent rather than being revealed in evolution or creation, even though God as the Word is said to have "become flesh and to have dwelt amongst us" (John 1:14).

The God Archetype

I shall begin with some definitions and comments on the nature of the so-called God archetype as this term has been used by Jung and his followers. On the basis of an extensive study of comparative religion and the dream content of his patients, Jung proposed the existence of what he referred to as a God archetype in *Aion* (1951). This was one of the archetypes of the collective unconscious and denoted timeless and universal symbols or images of the numinous and of internal states of Self integration, harmony, balance, and wholeness. Examples of such symbols included the mandalas appearing in the dreams of patients. Religious expressions of the God archetype included the awe-inspiring, cosmic mandalas represented in the rose windows of cathedrals like Chartres, the cross, and the eight-spoked wheel and lotus flower of Buddhism. A symbolic representation of the Christ figure or the Buddha often appeared at the center of such religious mandalas. The archetypes of death and rebirth, the hero, and the savior are also numinous in nature (see chapters 4 and 6 for further discussion of archetypal symbols of the numinous).

Before considering human experiences of the God archetype and the actual nature of this cosmic phenomenon, it is necessary to return briefly to the psychophysical problem and dispose of the implicit monist, reductionist materialism in the arguments used to dismiss God as a delusion. The philosophical position of metaphysical materialism is pervasive in contemporary Western thought, perhaps partly because the idea that reality is that which can be determined solely through observation utilizing the senses (or technologies that extend the senses) is so seductively plausible.

Metaphysical materialism is also a product of the mindlessness that was characteristic of both classical mechanistic physics and radical behaviorism in psychology. The latter theory embraced the philosophy of positivism enthusiastically. Thus, the mental fell into Wittgenstein's realm which "one must pass over in silence" so that the psyche was banished from psychology even as it was being rediscovered in quantum physics as the personal equation of the observer. Laurikainen, writing about this development in the correspondence of Wolfgang Pauli, comments on Newton: "a hesitancy appeared in his conception which eventually related to contradictions he had noticed to exist between the idea of absolute causality and religious concepts... awareness of this contradiction may have been the essential reason for the depression Newton underwent sometime after the publication of his *Principia*. At the time it became clear to Newton that his main work would be used to support materialism and atheism" (1988, 47). According to Pauli, "belief in the idea that God had created the world as perfect, able to be perfectly described, mathematically produced as an outcome a world picture in which God no longer has any place" (ibid., 49). In depth psychology, by contrast, the prevailing view was that without psyche there would be no theory, and this was consistent with Schrödinger's position that the whole of science was a construct of the mental.

The difficulty with monist materialism, which reduces the mental to the physical, is that it is a metaphysical doctrine about nature and not an explanation of nature as understood by empirical science. This doctrine, implicit in the teaching and understanding of science, regards the mental (and such concepts as God) as having no basis in reality or as being mere epiphenomenal by-products of brain processes, a position toward which Pribram (2004), for instance, is hostile. An epistemology that includes the mental is one in which the mystical or cosmic religious experience of the God archetype is not regarded as merely illusory or delusional in Dawkins's sense. Even materialists such as neuroscientist Vilayanur S. Ramachandran (1997) admit the possibility of a scientific study of religious experience, which he calls "neurotheology" and which assumes that such phenomena are to be identified with genetically encoded brain processes that can be observed using various imaging techniques such as functional magnetic resonance imaging (fMRI). The demonstration of a neural substrate for religious experience does not necessarily imply a reductionist identification of such phenomena with brain processes. By contrast in this book I argue for a position of dual aspect monism with regard to the mind-brain relationship as will be clear in my discussion of the work of Karl Pribram and Hiley and Pylkkänen among others.

Jungian analyst Michael Fordham, who perceived a relationship of correspondence between psychic and immune defense and who was influenced by psychoanalytic self psychology, wrote that "structures designed to receive messages directed toward preservation of the Self... are archetypes organized under the aegis of DNA" (1985, 167). However, this would assume that DNA itself is to be understood only in materialistic terms, an assumption that now seems quite dubious in view of the Bohm-Hiley concept of active information as a rudimentary mindlike quality at the quantum level and the complementarity of mind and matter. Both dualist interactionism and such dual aspect positions as the complementarity notion permit the predicate of existence to be attributed to mental events and processes without adopting a reductionist posture.

Once the mental is viewed autonomously and as existing from the quantum level through to the human experience of consciousness, eliminative materialism is exposed as an article of faith. These considerations will hopefully be sufficient to convince the reader that, metaphysics aside, the manifestations of the God archetype, amplified by Jung and his followers, can be regarded as a transhistorical and transcultural phenomenon worthy of scientific study.

In more general terms—and as Laurikainen, commenting on the collaboration between Jung and Pauli, has expressed it—"archetypes are expressions of a cosmic order which is verifiable both in our observations of the external world and in the structure of the internal world of our psyche.... The laws of nature of the physical world are in this way a physical expression of the archetypes. That ordering and regulating the archetypes is something in common to the structure of both the external world and that of the psyche" (1988, 149). It is a central thesis of this book that a world structured in this way is not possible without a "God" or numinous principle implicit in cosmology and evolution. However, this is certainly not the anthropomorphic projection of "God" derided by skeptics.

The manifestations of the God archetype (or God imago) in numinous or mystical experiences would also be expected to undergo evolution in parallel with the development of human consciousness, culture, and science, as Jung (1940), Teilhard de Chardin (1964), and Hans Küng (2007) have clearly perceived. However, such an implicit incarnational theology might be relevant to a humankind that has outgrown its infancy, while embracing the figurative quantum entanglement, holism, and interconnectedness of all beings necessary for its maturity and future survival. It is to such a concept of transcendence that I shall turn in arguing that it is humankind's *participation* in God that will further evolution as well as the survival of the species.

Evolution and Transcendence

The current historical period in the developed world has been referred to as the age of narcissism by psychoanalyst Heinz Kohut (1993). Narcissism entails not merely egocentricity, but also an attitude toward the world of arrogant self-entitlement, ruthlessness, and exploitativeness. Conversely, overcoming the narcissistic predicament requires becoming capable of empathy, creativity, humor, and wisdom. Mario Jacoby has made a similar point in *Individuation and Narcissism: The Psychology of Self in Jung and Kohut,* commenting upon the "goals of narcissistic maturation and their meaning for the individuation process" (1991, 113–134). Jacoby writes that "the centering forces from the unconscious are structured by the self and are often manifested through symbols conveying a numinous element" (ibid.,113). Thus the mirror of self-absorption is shattered, and the person becomes capable of perceiving the reality not only of other human beings, but also, potentially, the indivisible vastness and wholeness of the universe itself. If consumerism and greed are individual and collective manifestations of narcissistic pathology, then a concern for the human species and for the ecology that sustains it represents the beginning of a capacity for transcendence.

Narcissism necessarily limits or precludes such a capacity, just as it eclipses experience of the numinous. Put differently and to use theologian Martin Buber's (1988) phrase, narcissistic disorders result in an "eclipse of God" from consciousness because the ego has arrogated God to itself, becoming the grandiose center of its own devotion (Jacoby 1991). In brief, narcissism and mystical experience of a numinous reality beyond the self are mutually exclusive opposites.

As Kohut (1993) put it, narcissism is the enemy of creativity, just as it precludes awareness of a cosmic evolutionary process in which the individual can participate. Both heightened awareness of something that transcends the confines and finiteness of the ego and passionate participation in such a reality are necessary conditions for the numinous experience of something infinite to which the ego can relate. If, as Jung wrote in *Memories, Dreams, Reflections,* the most decisive question for humanity is whether we are "related to something infinite or not" (1961, 357), it may well be that phenomena such as mathematical insight or scientific illumination provide some people with affirmative answers.

However self-transcendence, or participation in God through contribution to an evolutionary process, is not limited to mathematicians or scientists. It necessarily includes musicians, artists, and writers who raise collective consciousness and act as catalysts for social transformation. It is an experience possible for any human being who has overcome the narcissistic predicament and who has achieved the necessary maturity to be concerned by challenges such as global warming and the HIV/AIDS pandemic in the developing world.

The techniques of civil disobedience and nonviolent protest pioneered by Mahatma Gandhi were used effectively to end apartheid in South Africa, and to enhance the civil rights of African Americans in the United States, and they contributed to ending U.S. involvement in the Vietnam War. The militant nationalism manifest in subsequent and ongoing wars in the Middle East could be construed as culturally or phylogenetically archaic and regressive.

These strategies promoted a form of negative or downward transcendence—the descent of humanity—rationalized by fundamentalist religious doctrines that promote divisiveness rather than an attitude of geopolitical holism and reverence for the earth which gives life to the species. Nothing short of a transformation of collective consciousness and a reawakening of a sense of the numinous in humanity as a whole will permit choices by which we will avoid the extinction of our species and the destruction of the earth. This is not merely a way of emphasizing the role of mind in directing evolution. It is an argument for consciousness and spirituality in countering the pernicious religion of metaphysical materialism and consumerism that represents a menace to the survival of all people.

Immortality and Self-Continuity

Entangled with curiosity about the existence of a numinous or supernatural dimension of being is a concern with the question of personal immortality or self-continuity after death. Metaphysical materialists tend to be derisive toward those who contemplate this ultimate question, considering them as being either unconsciously bound by some infantile residue of past religious indoctrination or simply antirational and unscientific. As a great pioneer in exploring the unconscious depths of the mind, Freud in such works as *The Future of an Illusion* (1927) regarded himself as an atheist and belief in immortality as due to a wish-fulfilling denial of death. Influenced by the mechanistic classical physics that had informed the epistemology of science since Newton and by the evolutionary theory of Charles Darwin, Freud viewed himself as both a rationalist and a materialist for whom all apparently mental phenomena would one day be explained by knowledge about brain processes. This project has been taken up in recent years by the field of neuropsychoanalysis, which has its own journal edited by Oliver Turnbull and David Olds. I shall return later to the question of whether subjective or phenomenological conscious experience can be predicted even from highly sophisticated brain scanning techniques.

Freud experienced occasional lapses in the form of speculations about the timelessness of the unconscious and whether symbolic dream content might not reveal some archaic residue of humankind's evolutionary past in the form of racial heredity or memories revealed to ego-consciousness. This brought him close to Jung's concept of the archetypes of the collective unconscious revealed in universal symbols (to be discussed in chapter 4). However, in spite of such apparent "slips" or indications of a perhaps unconscious theism, Freud viewed the dispelling of religious belief as an integral part of his scientific project of liberating humanity from superstition and magical thinking. This part of his project was detailed in such works as *Moses and Monotheism* (1939) and *The Future of an Illusion* (1927).

The illusion, of course, was religion with its irrational dogmas and beliefs in such notions as God and immortality. Richard Dawkins, who relies heavily upon Darwin and the doctrine of natural selection, might well consider Freud's works as secular scriptures supporting his God Delusion, if only Freud had treated the role of mind in evolution more seriously. Dawkins, surprisingly perhaps, does not quote Freud's published works on religion in *The God Delusion* (2006) directly, although they formed part of the zeitgeist of the twentieth century. In fact, he has little to say about depth psychology or unconscious and timeless dimensions of mind and of the Self. Wallace's conjecture that natural selection might not be a sufficient explanation of mind ought to have been a warning even if Dawkins ignores the field of depth psychology and decades of consciousness studies involving quantum physics as well as neuroscience.

The existence of rudimentary mindlike qualities even at the quantum level and the role of consciousness in emergent evolution are highly relevant to the continuity and immortality questions. If biosystems have discovered quantum computing in advance of humans, the neo-Darwinian theory of evolution, enshrined as scientific dogma for the past century, might itself have to undergo a major paradigm shift that allows Wallace's anomaly to be finally addressed. Clearly, Schrödinger and Pauli as well as more contemporary eminent physicists including Bohm and Penrose have taken the mind much more seriously than such writers as Dawkins. The solution of the psychophysical or mind-matter problem and that of self-continuity will entail considering contributions from all of these fields of enquiry.

Mind-matter anomalies such as near-death experiences, "which transcend the individual in a transpersonal sense," as described by physicist Harald Atmanspacher (2007, 133), may yield further insights as a result of empirical scientific research. This is a personally salient question due to my own self-transformative near-death experience in August 2005 during severe complications following triple bypass heart surgery. Phenomenologically, this was an experience in which my finite ego-consciousness felt connected to a rapturously beautiful Light, a loving Presence and Source of wisdom, which seemed to be infinite, cosmic, numinous, timeless, and eternal, not spatiotemporally bound and without any apparent beginning or end. The Light seemed to be far brighter than the external sun, boundless and all-enveloping. I was left with a profound sense of tasks to fulfill and contributions yet to be made to science and humanity, work which might contribute to furthering the work of those who had come before me, especially in depth psychology, psychoanalysis, and religion. Afterward, the world seemed to be pristine, renewed, resacralized, and transfigured in my consciousness. My first comment to a friend about the experience was, "God... is so beautiful!" The unconscious God archetype, which I seem to have encountered during the near-death experience, filled me with a sublime sense of the oceanic unity and wholeness of all people and faith traditions as well as the integration of science and religion. What I described as the Source became the inspiration for the work I have since published and presented, especially on depth psychology and the numinous dimension of evolutionary becoming. I have discussed the implications of this near-death experience and the notion that consciousness is not a mere causally inefficacious and epiphenomenal by-product of brain processes in "Unconscious Mental Factors in HIV Infection" (2008) and online (2011).

I conclude that such contributions, further elucidated through empirical research in neuropsychoanalysis to enhance understanding of the neural substrate of phenomenological experiences, not only provide intimations of continuity but point to the need to evolve the concept of a numinous dimension implicit in the evolutionary process and with it a twenty-first-century theology. First, however, I shall now turn to a more detailed discussion of collaborative work between quantum physicists and depth psychologists and the implications of the notion of a complementarity of mind and matter for the self-continuity issue. Timeless dimensions of the self and of the unconscious in depth psychology, as well as concepts of transpersonal meaning and purpose, are of particular relevance insofar as they imply breaking the spatiotemporal hold that has strangled attempts to grasp the mind-matter relationship.

Complementarity of Mind and Matter

Pauli considered that the relationship between mind and matter, like the distinction between living and nonliving systems, was a manifestation of Bohr's complementarity principle, so that one is not necessarily reducible to the other as occurs both in materialism and idealism. Bohm used the example of a magnet with north and south poles analogous to the wave particle duality of light. Schrödinger (1992) believed that the quantum laws manifest in the organization of matter—the emergence of living systems and, eventually, consciousness—implied the existence of something mindlike as an organizing principle. And as already noted, even the concepts of space and time are constructs of mind in Schrödinger's thought.

I shall discuss the relationship of mind to the so-called arrow of time and the spatiotemporal hold at the end of this chapter. If this argument means a long overdue vindication of the evolutionary views of Huxley and Teilhard de Chardin, the latter simply dismissed as "self-deceptive" by Dawkins (2006, 154), it would be much more ludicrous to make a similar assertion of deceit about a physicist as eminent as Nobel laureate Erwin Schrödinger or one as highly regarded as Roger Penrose, who wrote the foreword to the 1992 edition of Schrödinger's book, *What Is Life? With "Mind and Matter" and "Autobiographical Sketches."* Huxley, I would remind the reader, wrote the introduction to Teilhard's perhaps best-known book, *The Phenomenon of Man*, and, while not embracing Jesuit theology, nevertheless conveyed an attitude of the highest respect for the scientific integrity of the man who was such an evolutionary visionary.

Pauli's exclusion principle elegantly explained the order and complexity of elements on the periodic table, while organizational principles on the quantum level were explored by Bohm in both his ontological interpretation of quantum theory and his concept of an implicate order (2002, 384). I shall turn in the next sections to a greater amplification of the work of both Pauli and Bohm on the nature of mind. For the moment, however, I shall simply mention some additional comments made by Bohm in his final work, *The Undivided Universe* (2002), writing not only about the notion of the evolved consciousness of humanity reflecting the universe to itself but also of an "indefinitely extended" or infinite Mind (ibid., 386).

The expanded notion of mind which I have been exploring might well be an implicit if not as yet explicit assertion of a transcendent and numinous principle in evolution, though one which probably lies outside traditional theology in creating bridges between religion and diverse disciplines of science. It is also, I believe, one that nevertheless has unexpected implications for such questions as the existence of a numinous dimension and that of self-continuity. I could suggest, satirically perhaps, that Bohm was inspired by the "spirit" of Schrödinger, or by whatever it is that breathes fire into the equations of physicists!

The Contribution of Pauli: The U-field

Though using somewhat different languages, both Pauli and Bohm came to similar conclusions about the organization of matter from the perspective of quantum mechanics. Certainly, both physicists rejected materialist reductionism while embracing the notion of complementarity in elucidating the relationship between mind and matter, or the psychophysical problem. As I have already argued, the solution to this problem illuminates issues entangled with it, including questions of the existence of a numinous dimension of evolution and self-continuity.

Contrary to the objections of skeptical materialists, such questions can be passed over in silence, but not because they are beyond the domain of empirical science or incorrigible even to falsification. Such objections are themselves articles of the faith of metaphysical materialism, which simply prohibits the scientific treatment of notions such as self-continuity and the numinous on the basis of a doctrine of nature. This is another example of the familiar principle in the philosophy of science of doctrine precluding observation.

Pauli was concerned that science since the sixteenth century, with its notions of a totally detached observer, strict mechanistic determinism, and absolute causality, had so totally exorcised "spirit" from its investigations of nature that it had succumbed to a one-sided development and become unbalanced. Classical physics and a mechanistic (or "clockwork") universe had no room for the human observer or for the mind that nevertheless devised experiments and deduced elegant mathematical laws from them. As Schrödinger ironically observed, no personal God could be found in a space-time from which everything personal had been removed by a priori definition. Everything mental had been banished and would reappear only in a new quantum physics which accounted for the observer in the form of the personal equation.

In fact, neither classical physics nor Darwin's theory of evolution could explain mind or consciousness, with the result that mental qualities were either squeezed out of existence or dismissed as mere causally inefficacious and epiphenomenal by-products of brain processes. Like Wallace, Pauli regarded this anomaly as troublesome, particularly as scientific theories themselves were "products of the psyche" with a great deal of "unconscious preparation," as noted in Laurikainen's book on the correspondence between Wolfgang Pauli and physicist Markus E. Fierz. Laurikainen wrote, "Archetypes are mysterious factors in the unconscious region of the psyche which arrange sensory stimuli according to certain patterns and thus create man's picture of the universe" (1988, 148–149). Pauli had noted that in quantum experiments the so-called personal equation or consciousness of the observer could no longer be ignored, and probably as a result of his collaboration with Carl Jung, he concluded that repression of the psyche "after the seventeenth century has been one-sided and dangerous," creating "a materialistic culture where the influence of religion has continuously diminished and of which a strict separation between science and religion is characteristic" (in Laurikainen 1988, xv).

The return (or one might say revenge) of what had been repressed could be said to be the explosions resulting from nuclear fission and such epidemics of irrationality and mass psychopathology as that observed during the Third Reich with its own dark god in the form of Hitler himself. This epidemic of madness, which engulfed Europe and threatened the very existence of civilization, was no delusion. It can be understood, in part at least, as an unintended consequence of metaphysical materialism, as could the mass murders committed under Stalin in the former Soviet Union and the events ordered by Chairman Mao during the Cultural Revolution in China.

Pauli regarded the psychophysical problem as one of the greatest challenges confronting science and philosophy, and, as I have already intimated, he viewed the relationship between mind and matter as one of complementarity and the archetypes as cosmic ordering and regulating principles. For Pauli, the archetypes combine sensory stimuli forming certain outlines, and in this way a picture of the world is formed corresponding to the properties of the human psyche. The bridge that the archetypes form between our theoretical concepts and the regularities of the external world lies hidden in the unconscious, "as if beneath a veil" (in Laurikainen 1988, 149). With his concept of a U-field, Pauli regarded the unconscious as the psychological analogy to the concept of the physical field, except that the U-field was not spatiotemporally bound (von Meyenn 2011, 11).

Apropos the quantum world, for both Pauli and Heisenberg the so-called wave function referred to the observer's knowledge, and observation itself was considered to be an interaction between the material object and the consciousness of the observer, resulting in a collapse of the wave function and hence information about the status of the particle.

One archetype that was particularly meaningful to Pauli was known as the *coniunctio oppositorum*, the union of opposites or wholeness, reflected in the nonlocal effects, interconnectedness, and holism associated with both the quantum situation and the unconscious psyche. The symbols of wholeness and Self integration arising from the unconscious were indistinguishable from those associated with the God image or God archetype and awakened feelings of a distinctly religious or mystical nature. The mathematically describable regularities with which Pauli was concerned were responsible for the increasing states of complexity, order, and self-organization manifest eventually in the evolution of life.

The Jungian unconscious refers to an "invisible reality mediating a connection between spatially and temporally distant phenomena" (von Meyenn 2011). Such a concept simply explicates the complementarity relationship between mind and matter in an epistemological dual aspect, monist position (Todd 2011, 14). Pauli's cosmic ordering principles or archetypes were not spatiotemporally bound or confined. They were as universal, timeless, or eternal as those which, like God, belonged to Jung's collective unconscious, particularly when identified with both the external universe and the so-called cosmos within, a term which would perhaps have created rapturous emotion for scientists with mystical tendencies and a capacity for cosmic religious feelings

like Teilhard de Chardin and even Einstein himself. Levels of mind
and influences that are independent of space and time are the very
stuff of which numinous experience of the God archetype (or image)
are made, while being of direct relevance to advancing the theological
idea of an evolving God. Atmanspacher and Primas have observed that
in addition to his contribution to understanding the psychophysical
problem, Pauli was particularly interested in biological evolution.
They note that Pauli was skeptical that the evolution of life could be
explained only by the natural selection of random mutations. Quoting
from Pauli's correspondence with Niels Bohr, they write, "In discus-
sions with biologists I met with difficulties when they apply the concept of natural selection in a rather wide field without being able to
estimate the probability of the occurrence, in an empirically given time,
of just those events which have been important for biological evolution.
Treating the empirical time scale of the evolution theoretically as
infinity, they have an easy game apparently to avoid the concept of
purposiveness. While they pretend to stay in this way completely
scientific and rational" (Atmanspacher and Primas 2006, 27–28).
Nonrandom or directed mutations, the U-field, and the existence of
finality (purposiveness) in evolution would be consistent with the
existence of an unconscious "God" principle implicit in the evolutionary
process while constituting a challenge to dogmatic neo-Darwinism.

How such an apparently unconscious God becomes conscious
through incarnation in humanity is a question to which I shall turn
after discussing Bohm's contribution to science and religion.

The Implicate Order of Bohm

David Bohm, in his later work, evolved a concept of mind that closely
resembled that of Pauli and Jung, especially the concept of the collective
unconscious. In *Wholeness and the Implicate Order* (1980), Bohm wrote
of what he referred to as "the vast unconscious background of explicit
consciousness, and ultimately unknowable depths of inwardness,
analogous to the sea of energy which fills the sensibly perceived empty
space" (1980, 267). Like Pauli, Bohm employed wholeness and found
that influences independent of space and time were needed in quantum
physics. By the time Bohm completed his final work, *The Undivided
Universe* (2002), he had come to the insight that "active information
served as a bridge between the mental and the physical" (2002, 386).

Information contained in thought, he wrote, is simultaneously a related neurophysiological activity (ibid.).

Bohm's concept of active information as a bridge between mind and matter is very similar to Pauli's notion of the unconscious archetypes as cosmic ordering and regulating principles providing such a bridging function in arguing for a relationship of complementarity between mind and matter. The number archetypes are among the most basic in the Jung/Pauli concept of complementarity. And Bohm clearly adopted a dual aspect notion of the mental and the physical as being complementary to one another while rejecting reductionism of either an idealist or materialist nature. Like Pauli, he avoided a misplaced faith in the religion of either metaphysical materialism or panpsychism. More controversially perhaps, Bohm postulated human participation in "a greater collective mind, in principle capable of going indefinitely beyond even the human species as a whole" (2002, 386). He might just as well have spoken of participation in God, perhaps a God becoming conscious through evolved humanity.

Bohm summed up his position concerning the role of the observer, again in a way that closely resembles Pauli, concluding, "There is no need to regard the observer as basically separate from what he sees nor to reduce him to an epiphenomenon of the objective process. More broadly one could say that through the human being, the universe has created a mirror to observe itself" (2002, 389). Such reflections on mind not only represent a case against metaphysical materialism, they also, I believe, refute Dawkins's argument that God is a "delusion."

The God that Dawkins and other skeptics regard as a delusion is the immutable designer of the static pre-Copernican universe, a God created in the image of humanity on the basis of anthropomorphic projection and the creative imagination of artists such as Michaelangelo. As I have already pointed out, this God was assassinated by the physics of Newton as well as by the evolutionary theory of Darwin, so Dawkins's deicide is both futile and irrelevant to a scientifically illuminated theology. Bohm's system of thought, however, may be a valuable contribution to such a theology.

Thinking like that of Pauli and Schrödinger could indeed help lay the foundations for a theology of the third millennium. In this new theology, humanity, as Teilhard predicted, not only participates in something numinous but also completes God by becoming fully conscious and directing the future evolution of the biosphere and noosphere. This would be an unfolding process that contains Mind even at the level of the infinitesimal, in the form of active information, until a summit of complexity, order, and central organization in the matter of the human brain is reached in which evolution becomes reflectively conscious of itself, programming the brain to create culture. I shall now turn to the question of God becoming conscious and requiring humanity in order to become whole and complete in the cosmic evolutionary process. This conceptualizes a theology to replace that which, as Jung noted in *Modern Man in Search of a Soul* (1933), was losing its meaning for humanity. Jung explores the notion of God becoming conscious and complete through incarnation in humanity in "Answer to Job" (1952a) to which I shall be referring in what follows.

God Becoming Conscious

Some of the statements of Pauli, Bohm, and Jung, as well as those whose contributions I shall explore, almost suggest a tendency to identify mind, in its unconscious aspects, with either an archetypal source of numinous experience or with a God immanent in matter itself. Jung, in such sources as *Memories, Dreams, Reflections* (1961) and "Answer to Job" (1952a), quite specifically writes of the evolution of God according to the archetype of the *coniunctio oppositorum* or wholeness. As the following passages demonstrate, in so doing, Jung seems to be treating God (and Christianity) as a patient in analysis for whom consciousness needs to be brought into his unconscious darkness in a self-transformative process.

In "Answer to Job," Jung documents what he believes to be God's less than respectable "shadow" qualities, needing to be integrated into the "light" of consciousness as would those of a patient with a bipolar mood disorder or one presenting sociopathic tendencies who had come to Jung for psychotherapy. As a patient, however, God is clearly identified by Jung both as a phenomenon of the collective unconscious, that is, as an archetype and as being coextensive with a cosmos which was evolving long before the origins of life and the eventual emergence of humanity.

Insofar as God's more archaic qualities correspond to phylogenetic stages of evolution that existed prior to human civilization, perhaps mood swings, irascibility, jealousy, and rage should not be surprising unless one succumbs to the temptation, so evident in orthodox

Christianity, of identifying God only with the "light" or higher consciousness associated with the theological Christ. For instance, in the Gospel of St. John (1:1–14) God as the Word made flesh is identified with both the Light of the divine and with Christ. However, it is precisely this expanded and higher consciousness which Jung believes God acquires through incarnation in humankind, the species in which reflective consciousness in its most sublime form emerged. It is in this sense, too, that Jung has expressed the belief that God needs humankind to become both whole and complete. These arguments are illustrated by the following quotations from Jung's "Answer to Job."

Jung writes, "One should make it clear to oneself what it means when God becomes man. It means nothing less than a world-shaking transformation of God. It means more or less what creation meant in the beginning, namely an objectivation of God. At the time of creation he revealed himself in nature; now he wants to be more specific and become man" (1952a, 401). Jung refers to the human as well as the divine nature of Christ, alluding to the "despairing cry from the cross, My God, My God, why hast thou forsaken me? Here his human nature attains divinity; at that moment God experiences what it means to be a mortal man and drinks to the dregs what he has made his faithful servant Job suffer. Here is given the answer to Job and clearly this supreme moment is as divine as it is human as eschatological as it is psychological" (ibid., 408).

Jung amplified the significance of God becoming human further: "God's incarnation in Christ requires continuation and completion because Christ owing to his virgin birth and his sinlessness was not an empirical human being at all. As stated in the first chapter of St. John, he represented a light which though it shone in the darkness was not comprehended by the darkness. He remained outside and above mankind" (ibid., 414). Finally, Jung envisions an evolution in the *imago Dei* through historic time: "the future indwelling of the Holy Ghost in man amounts to a continuing incarnation of God, Christ as the begotten son of God and pre-existing mediator is a first born and a divine paradigm which will be followed by further incarnations of the Holy Ghost in the empirical man" (ibid., 432). Through ongoing incarnation in humanity God becomes conscious and is completed by humankind in directed evolution.

It is as an archetypal and cosmic reality that the concept of an evolving God seems to be most compatible with those notions of rudimentary mind mentioned above in the contributions from quantum physics such as those of Pauli and Bohm. I shall now consider in some detail the work of Bohm's colleague Basil Hiley on mind as active information and the contribution of mathematician Hans Primas on the nature of time, to move toward a deeper understanding of the intelligibility of the notion of an "unconscious" God immanent in the universe.

As theologian Hans Küng (2007) has put it, God is both in the world and greater than it, though, I would add, requiring an expanded consciousness through incarnation in humanity. Again, such a transformation of God would be analogous to the process of making the unconscious conscious, which characterizes analytically oriented psychotherapies. These reflections in turn may yield both a concept of the numinous and a theology appropriate to the third millennium.

Hiley and Pylkkänen (2005) articulate Bohm's ontological interpretation of quantum theory in such a way as to suggest that a new type of active information connected with a novel type of quantum potential energy could enhance understanding of how mental processes can act on traditional classically describable neural processes without violating the energy conservation law. According to Hiley, hidden commitments to classical physics may unnecessarily constrain neuroscience while leaving the neural basis of meaning, intentionality, creativity, and intelligence in a scientific limbo. Penrose (1999, 2004) has referred to analogous nonalgorithmic and noncomputable aspects of intelligence such as those manifest in creativity and original mathematical insights. Hiley and Pylkkänen believe that quantum potential energy is some form of "internal energy" that contains information about the environment in which the particle finds itself in the experimental situation (2005, 19).

Bohm's implicate order enfolds information about the whole environment at each region of space and enables nonlocal correlations to exist between particles. It also provides a framework for understanding the relationship between mind and matter in a way that is describable mathematically. These characteristics of the implicate order, similar to those of archetypes as cosmic ordering and regulating principles, extends understanding of the unconscious, which has been taken up for instance by Primas (2003) whose ideas concern a time entanglement between mind and matter as realities complementary to one another.

Schrödinger wrote an entire essay (1992) on the role of quantum laws and processes in the emergence of life, mind, and eventually of consciousness. He also wrestled with the notion of the spatiotemporal hold of classical physics and questioned whether the "arrow of time" was capable of destroying the mind that had constructed it. This, of course, remains one of the ultimate mysteries to which a third millennium theology will need to address itself without regressing to the fantasies and mythology of world destruction depicted in the biblical book of Revelation. Revelation is still interpreted literally by religious fundamentalists, including, most alarmingly, some world leaders with the political power and shadow qualities to make such dark, apocalyptic myths a reality.

The Mind Field

According to Hiley and Pylkkänen, the majority of cognitive neuroscientists have regarded the brain solely in terms of classical concepts, ignoring the notion of active information as represented in the Bohm model. One notable exception was neuroscientist and Nobel laureate John Eccles, who postulated that what he called a "mind field" could affect neural firing at a quantum level, proposing that quantum effects control the frequency of exocytosis (release of neurotransmitters or chemical messengers) at the synaptic cleft between neurons. The chief materialist objection to this proposition was that any such effect of a nonmaterial mind would violate the conservation of energy principle.

To counter this apparently fatal objection, Hiley and Pylkkänen suggested viewing the mind field as an emergent property in biological systems that have reached a certain level of organization and complexity. Here, Hiley and Pylkkänen, like Bohm, deploy a dual aspect monist perspective on the mind-matter problem, so that mind and matter are simply two ways of looking at an underlying reality. The mind field containing active information, with its mental and physical aspects as complementary to one another, is also situated within a broader context of field theories of consciousness (including that of Penrose with his notion of quantum gravity–induced collapse of the wave function).

The point of departure for the model proposed by Hiley and Pylkkänen is the already mentioned suggestion that even the quantum level can be thought to have, via active information, a primitive mindlike quality, though without consciousness (thus avoiding the error of panpsychism). According to this model, quantum processes trigger some neural processes in the brain, but these in turn can be affected by some higher-level process such as the mind field, which is a higher level of organization, again with both a mental and a physical aspect.

At each level, information (putting form into process) is the link or bridge between the mental and physical sides. The conclusion of this argument is as follows:

> Mind regarded as a process taking place at a higher level of organization with both a mental and a physical aspect goes beyond processes studied in traditional neuroscience but can nevertheless play an active role in the physical world. Through its effect, for example, on exocytosis Mind is now understood as a new level containing active information which affects the quantum potential which in turn affects the physical processes in the brain. (Hiley and Pylkkänen 2005, 23)

As Hiley and Pylkkänen concluded, it was necessary to go beyond the standard quantum theory to make approaches such as that of Eccles coherent. The factor beyond the notion of quantum effects triggering neural processes in the brain is that the active information contained in Eccles's mind field can in turn affect the quantum potential. Thus, according to Hiley and Pylkkänen, mind can be viewed as a relatively autonomous, though higher, level of active information, the mental and physical aspects of which stand in a relationship of complementarity, so that mind can have a genuine effect on neural processes. I shall extend these notions further by discussing the contributions of mathematician Hans Primas and neuroscientist Karl Pribram in later chapters.

The Arrow of Time and Mind

Hans Primas (2003) takes Pauli's idea that mind and matter are complementary aspects of the same reality as his point of departure. As a working hypothesis, he begins with the undivided, timeless, primordial reality (the *unus mundus* or one world), the original symmetry of which is broken into two domains, one tensed, the other tenseless. In Primas's proposal, the tensed domain includes nonmaterial processes and mental events. The tenseless domain refers to matter and physical energy. The implication is that neither mind nor matter can be reduced to one another. Thus, Primas rejects any form of mindless reductionism from the outset. Tensed concepts are generated by relating events to the present and include the properties of pastness, nowness, and futurity, whereas tenseless concepts are generated by the relations earlier than, simultaneous with, and later than.

These conceptual distinctions correspond to the psychological or inner experience of time or of the flow of mental events, on the one hand, and the external time of physical events and processes, of which the special relativity theory is an example, on the other hand. (The question of self-continuity needs to be considered with this distinction in mind, a point which I shall take up when considering the contribution of Pribram with his related notion of pre-spacetime.)

It is here that the timeless viewpoint of depth psychology becomes important. Primas, turns especially to the work of Jung who maintained that in the deeper layers of the unconscious, no time exists at all, calling the factors responsible for the organization of unconscious psychic processes "archetypes." For Jung and Pauli, both space and time were manifestations of archetypal elements of the collective unconscious and hence psychic in origin. One implication of this insight is that the Self cannot be confined to space-time coordinates. Furthermore, the notion of continuity needs to be disentangled from this framework or conceptual prison of a spatiotemporal hold, which is itself a product of conscious rationality. Since both the mental and material domains are governed by common ordering principles (of a cosmic, archetypal nature), they are both complementary aspects of the same holistic reality.

Accordingly, Primas argues that we relate the tensed domain to a mental world that is fundamental to the nature of existence and being. Mind, however, operates as a principle beyond individual consciousness and is not restricted to the human mind or to the differentiation of the mental domain into individual, conscious egos. If the Self in its deeper unconscious or timeless, eternal aspect is not bound by space and time, then its continuity is not necessarily broken once the prison of the spatiotemporal hold is thrown open at death.

Perhaps self-continuity is not the illusion that confinement of the mind by the constructions of space and time would strongly suggest. This is a view that Jung himself seems to have entertained, at least as an afterthought, in *Memories, Dreams, Reflections* (1961). However, this is the question of whether the arrow of time strikes a mortal blow to its own creator, which I shall treat extensively in chapter 6. At this point, I will consider Pribram's reassessment of consciousness with its notion that current physics is rooted in both matter and mind, given that mathematics, which describes the relationships organizing matter, is a psychological process. Mathematical epiphanies and such rapturously beautiful insights and solutions as those of Schrödinger and Einstein seem to be discoveries of eternal truths rather than inventions, as Penrose (2004), for instance, has suggested.

CHAPTER 4

Consciousness as an Organizing Principle

I have thus far argued that such notions as Bohm's implicate order and the concept of archetypes as cosmic ordering and regulating principles give primacy to mind, especially in its active informational aspects, in the organization of matter into ever increasing states of complexity necessary for the evolutionary emergence of life and ultimately of consciousness. Indeed, mind understood in such terms extends not only beyond the collective consciousness of humanity. It encompasses the vastness of the cosmos itself from an internalist perspective. As a manifestation of such, human consciousness is not merely an epiphenomenal by-product of brain processes, because as Pribram reminds us, "the pen is so often mightier than the sword" (2004, 23).

An epiphenomenon that is also causally inefficacious could not evolve Popper and Eccles's (1983) World 3 of culture and science or seek the understanding of its own origins, meaning, or place in the universe. Pribram (2004, 29) uses the term *spiritual* to refer to the fact that conscious experience is attracted to patterns or "informational structures" that extend beyond immediate daily (or egocentric) concerns, like those of humankind's prehominid ancestors who pursued lives oriented primarily toward hunting and gathering, fulfilling basic needs, and survival rather than evolving meaning and culture. Such structures can be those of quantum physics, mathematics, neo-Darwinian evolution, or even the transcendent, religious systems of belief that Dawkins seems to be so willing to dismiss as "dangerous" obstacles to humankind's further ascent.

Even more profoundly, as Pribram notes, the World 2 of conscious-ness and mentality, in actively creating such World 3 structures as sci-ence and culture, has in turn established an evolutionary organization for developing both the brain and complex social organization. In other words, a feedback loop exists between Worlds 1, 2, and 3 so that the products of mind as expressed in language and culture, when encoded in material forms, in turn are utilized to stimulate brain development. Consciousness emerges as an organizing principle responsible for the future direction of cultural and scientific evolution. Such organization can be expressed, for instance, in mathematical laws and systems that begin as World 2 (mental) insights and, when encoded in such World 3 products as textbooks, become capable in turn of stimulating mind and enriching synaptic connections in the World 1 matter of human brains.

In this sense, and as Teilhard de Chardin saw so clearly, evolution has become both conscious of itself and directed, manifesting the very self-organizing mechanisms that sustain its upward and forward movement. Such an epiphany into the heart of matter is analogous to the discovery that understanding the symbolic significance of a cathedral, as Pribram (2004) suggests, is not limited to a mere grasp of the nature of the bricks of which it is constructed. A symbolic meaning is encoded in the structure as a whole that transcends any understanding of the composition of the bricks used in its construction.

Initially a product of the mental World 2, the cathedral belongs in its material aspect to both World 1 (the bricks) and World 3 (the history and theological beliefs encoded as information in its structure). Similar points could be made about such cultural artifacts as scientific theories, musical compositions, and other systems of thought (to use one of David Bohm's terms) which begin as Archimedean experiences of sometimes rapturous illumination or insight. (Such insights are not mere epiphenomena.)

These examples serve to illustrate the poverty of eliminative materialism as a doctrine of mind. The notion of three worlds of culture, brain, and mind has been explored most recently by Roger Penrose (2004, 1029) as well as Popper in his collaboration with Eccles. The notion of consciousness as an organizing principle in evolution has many implications for a God hypothesis and for refuting Dawkins's crude thesis of a God delusion. It is reflective consciousness that, in illuminating the darkness of our phylogenetic past and of the universe itself, sets humankind apart from all other species, creating an unbridgeable chasm between humanity and the animal world. Conscious experience itself is the beginning, not the end, of knowing and understanding. As Pribram put it, "through consciousness, we become related to each other and to the biological and physical universe and just as gravity relates material bodies, so consciousness relates sentient bodies" (2004, 11).

Pribram, like Pauli, Bohm, and Hiley, regards mind and matter as complementary manifestations of an underlying unity, which he refers to variously as "holoflux" or spectra of energy and momentum measured in terms of frequency (or spectral density) existing in pre-spacetime (2004, 13). Irrespective of the differences in language, the original or underlying reality is conceptually very similar to the timeless and primordial implicate order of Bohm and archetypal dimension of Jung and Pauli. Because the psychological process of mathematics describes relationships organizing matter, Pribram argues, there is a nontrivial sense in which current physics is rooted in both matter and mind, which have a common ontological root, specifically, a pre-spacetime potential that transcends spacetime (ibid., 14). In higher levels of organization, meaning no longer resides in the arrangement of simple elements (like bits), but in the "complexity of the pattern" (ibid., 15).

Underlying both brain and psychological processes is the holoflux. Transformations of this flux into spacetime coordinates specify material and temporal locations of information and meaning while being a more precise rendering of information processing by the brain. To return to Popper and Eccles's conjectures, interaction between the three worlds is necessary to achieve consciousness. The cultural effects of mentation, including new technologies and linguistic usages, feedback upon the brain, and the consequent brain processes feed forward onto evolving culture. This is reminiscent of the upward and forward movement described by Teilhard de Chardin (1964) in his discussion of the evolution of the collective consciousness of his noosphere. Hans Küng writes of the "spiritual cosmos" as one which shapes neuronal processes (2007, 189). This formulation is remarkably close to Pribram's notion that "the cultural world is spiritual" (2004, 29) and to the idea that far from being an epiphenomenon, consciousness programs the brain.

The problem with epiphenomenalism is that there is so much evidence against it: language creates revolutions in systems of thought (including scientific ones); the musical instruments we imagine and create, as well as compositions, move others to contemplation and rapture and, sometimes, to act upon the world. Reflectively conscious human beings, unlike our primate cousins, do not simply react passively to the environment or adapt to it. This is what led to Wallace's problem with the evolutionary significance of mind in creating culture. Action upon the world is mediated by reflection in conscious thought, and as Pribram concludes, "ineffable mind (minding) is replaced by communication" represented in culture (2004, 30).

For Pribram, the cultural world is spiritual in the sense already alluded to, namely, that conscious experience is irrevocably and magnetically drawn to patterns or informational structures beyond (transcending) those immediate daily concerns by which all other species are bound. As Jung (1961) phrased it, the most decisive question for a person is whether he or she is related to something infinite or not. Quantum physics, mathematics, depth psychology, music, and (shockingly) even theology stripped of primitive animism and anthropomorphisms are examples of Pribram's transcendent informational structures. However, such structures themselves evidence a Mind beyond that of the aggregate of individual human egos and which can be identified with Jung's collective unconscious and Pauli's U-field, discussed in chapter 3.

Quantum Computing, Biosystems, and the Beginnings of Life

While the weak version of the anthropic principle specifies the conditions necessary for the existence of life and sentient, conscious beings (Penrose, 2004, 760–762), the mystery of the origins of life remains one of the unsolved riddles of science. Dawkins objects strongly to the notion of intelligent design and the intervention of a divine creator as an explanation. Yet it is understandable how such erroneous doctrines have arisen as humankind attempted to explain its own existence to itself and given that, as Davies (2004, 75) and others have pointed out, it would have taken much longer than the entire age of the universe for even a single protein to have formed by chance from some form of primordial or prebiotic "soup," as discussed in chapter 2.

Current estimates, however, are that primitive life forms (perhaps molecular self-replicators like RNA) probably emerged about 4 billion years ago. If this estimate is accurate, it invalidates Dawkins's position that, given sufficient time, even extremely improbable events can and will occur as simply by chance. Even the estimated age of the universe of 13 billion years is still insufficient time for life, particularly in its current complexity and diversity, to have emerged. As Atmanspacher and Primas have noted, in discussing Pauli's ideas on purposiveness in evolution, "the claim that final processes are impossible is a dogmatic metaphysical preconception that should not be accepted uncritically" (2006, 32).

Once life begins, the neo-Darwinian principle of the natural selection of chance variations becomes applicable, although this paradigm has already been challenged by contributions to the understanding of biosystems from quantum physicists, in particular the existence of nonrandom or directed mutations. Quantum mechanics may help to solve the time problem without any need to resort to the primitive notion of intervention whereby God somehow beamed life into inanimate matter. The actual solution to the puzzle of the origins of life may be much more ingenious, involving quantum computing or information processing discovered by nature in advance of any such invention by human beings.

This scientifically tenable explanation would not require concepts such as mere randomness to do so much explanatory work, and information processing would move beyond the classical "bit" to encompass such complex patterns and recognition processes as are in fact observed in the behavior of biosystems. Even at the molecular level rapidly mutating microorganisms such as HIV exist at the interface of the living and the nonliving. Niels Bohr viewed the distinction between the living and the nonliving as an example of his complementarity principle, as noted by Laurikainen (1988, 204), while Schrödinger (1992) believed that quantum effects and laws could be manifest in the origins of life as well as producing mutations once life has begun.

The problem with traditional theological explanations of the origins of life is that some external, supernatural agency has been invoked as the cause. Dawkins rightly rejects such simplistic and animistic notions. The position I am elucidating here, however, views life as emerging from within matter that has reached a critical level of complexity, order, and central organization, perhaps with the assistance of some form of quantum computing or information processing at work as an internal aspect of matter itself.

This is conceived as an aspect of the unfolding of Bohm's implicate order or of the operation of the Jung/Pauli archetypes as cosmic ordering and regulating principles, prior to the later emergence of human consciousness through which the universe reflects upon itself and articulates its laws in mathematical equations. Such a view of the origins of life has no need of an external God. It describes a numinous or transcendent principle intrinsic to the programming of life in the matter of which the universe is composed. This position is consistent with process theology and the views of Teilhard de Chardin (1959,

1964). When human beings invent quantum computing, they might well have discovered a tool already present in nature.

Confusing the Hardware with the Software

Dawkins's rejection of theism is facilitated by a fundamental confusion in genetics and molecular biology. This is the confusion between what Davies (2004, 70) has described as the hardware or structural aspects of molecules and those which pertain to their software and are informational in nature. In biology the informational molecules are RNA and DNA, which have been considered from a predominantly classical or externalist perspective since the discovery of DNA by Watson and Crick in 1953. As Penrose, Davies, and others have pointed out, although quantum mechanics has been considered crucial to the structure of these molecules, it has been disregarded with respect to their information processing role. This neglect has resulted in the marginalization of any serious exploration of an internalist view of matter and of life. If it were found that biological systems do process information quantum mechanically, they would gain a marked advantage in speed and power, an advantage within the paradigm of natural selection.

Elucidating this internalist-ecological perspective, for instance by considering the contributions of Matsuno, McFadden, and Al-Khalili, might be sufficient to suggest that the quantum revolution in physics must eventually be mirrored in biology. McFadden and Al-Khalili (1999), for instance, have outlined a quantum mechanical model of adaptive mutation in direct challenge to neo-Darwinism. They applied this model to the understanding of multiple drug resistance in *Mycobacterium tuberculosis* and, while acquiring some preliminary supportive data, were unable to pursue the research due to a lack of funds (personal communication with McFadden, Tuesday, August 14, 2007, concerning possible quantum mechanical effects on the emergence of drug resistance). According to McFadden and Al-Khalili, living cells could act as biological quantum computers with a capacity to explore multiple mutational states simultaneously and select those states which "provide the greatest advantage" (1999, 210).

Such revolutionary science could mean a paradigm shift in the neo-Darwinian theory of evolution itself, whereby mind as active information would be given its proper place, rather than being ignored or dismissed as a mere epiphenomenon. Wallace's objection would no longer be disregarded, and confusing the software with the hardware would no longer be a permissible error. To reject this science could be construed as a perverse refusal to look at the inconvenient truth of Feynman's dictum that whatever technology humans invent, nature has already discovered, for example, quantum computing being exploited by biosystems. Matsuno's question was "Who got there first, biosystems or Richard Feynman?" (2000, 39).

It is very convenient for eliminative materialists and skeptics like Dawkins and Shermer to cling to conscious or unconscious investments in classical physics in their treatment of the phenomena of life and consciousness. As Newton discovered to his dismay, the mathematical laws of classical physics permit dispensing with any theological concept of God as a causal agency external to the universe composed of heavenly bodies in motion. Newton not only became depressed, at least partly because of this scientific "revelation" which apparently rendered God superfluous as I have already noted; he also managed to obtain for himself an exemption from ordination as a minister of the Church of England, which at the time was a condition of appointment to a professorial chair at Cambridge.

Dawkins has granted himself a similar dispensation by writing on the basis of two potent emotional investments: one is an investment in classical, mechanistic physics rather than post-relativity and quantum physics, the other is in strict neo-Darwinism and the religion of chance in the evolution of species. In so doing, the anomaly of mind can either be postponed for later consideration under the heading of memetics or simply ignored as the purely linguistic problem, which philosopher Bertrand Russell considered it to be.

In the post–quantum mechanical era, such indulgences are both scientifically slothful and deceitful, because quantum laws demand an internalist understanding of matter and in particular of life and biosystems. Dawkins imputes such deceit or self-deception to Teilhard de Chardin (2006, 154), as noted earlier. The real deception, however, belongs to Dawkins himself, who can argue persuasively for his God Delusion only by willfully ignoring the implications for evolution of the probable quantum mechanical underpinnings of the origins of life and mutation as well as consciousness. The Kuhnian anomaly for dogmatic neo-Darwinism, for instance, is of mutation perhaps being determined by quantum rather than classical laws as well as existing in nonrandom or adaptive forms.

I have discussed this anomaly already (for instance, in chapter 3), exploring Hiley and Pylkkänen's (2005) idea of mind as "active information" at the quantum level. Dawkins's deception, I am arguing, is his intelligent design of the illusion that the numinous can be considered only within the outdated and outmoded frameworks in both physics and biology. His God had already been eliminated as a superfluous entity by Newton and is not even a distant cousin to notions of the transcendent, which reflect knowledge of the "within" of matter, as Teilhard de Chardin has put it in *The Phenomenon of Man* (1959), or of mind as this phenomenon has been understood in quantum physics and contemporary neuroscience as well as depth psychology. Dawkins's argument is rooted in a defective, simplistic, and outmoded understanding of theology.

It is to more sophisticated modes of conceptualizing God that I shall now turn, mindful that such definitions of God as the "ground of all being" and as somehow immanent (implicate) in evolution emerged during the twentieth century in works as diverse as those of Martin Buber, Hans Küng, and John Shelby Spong, who tried to liberate the Christian Gospels from archaic literalism and anthropomorphism. Teilhard de Chardin's unorthodox incarnational theology implied some form of unfolding of the numinous from within matter itself, in a manner that in retrospect seems to me to be remarkably compatible with the quantum mechanical notions which I have been exploring.

For Teilhard de Chardin, the incarnation of God in the historic figure of Christ is itself an evolutionary "emergent" phenomenon, not necessarily the intervention of a remote God. His theology is of a revelation to humanity of the divinity to be awakened and realized in human beings, responsible for the future of the noosphere (the envelope of meaning and consciousness which enfolds the earth) and of cultural evolution. This is a radically different concept of the continuing incarnation of God, but one which grasps Christ as immanent and among us as well as transcendent and expressing a numinous archetype.

Teilhard de Chardin's silencing by a pre-Vatican II Catholic Church might well have been due to his emphasis upon the immanence of his God in Christogenesis and an apparent downplaying of a version of transcendence that retains residues of an external Creator still moulded in anthropomorphic imagery and a pre-Copernican immutable cosmos. The theme that in cultural evolution God becomes human in order for humanity to participate in God is one that I shall develop further in outlining a theology appropriate to the third millennium, illuminated by both quantum physics and the depth psychological understanding of the unconscious and the archetypes (see chapter 6). In his prosecution of the case for a God delusion, Dawkins is not only bound by the articles of faith encoded in classical physics and neo-Darwinism; he seems to hope that theologically naïve readers will not perceive the illusion he himself is creating under the guise of demolishing intelligent design and replacing it with a concept of natural selection, which as a theory of almost everything including cosmology and multiple universes conducive to the emergence of sentient beings (2006, 146) explains practically nothing at all about the origins of life and consciousness or the numinosity to be found in humanity itself.

Does a Case for God Still Exist?

Bohm's notion of the implicate order and Jung's and Pauli's concepts of the archetypes as cosmic ordering and regulating principles imply a form of epiphany or revelation to human consciousness of organizing principles that transcend both the aggregate of human egos and the collective consciousness of humankind. It is this reality that transcends the ego-consciousness to which it is revealed and which nevertheless participates in it. I shall refer to this as God insofar as it is experienced subjectively as Other and as bound neither by spacetime nor by the confines of the ego.

This transcendent reality has neither a beginning nor an end in a temporal sense; it emerges from the timeless and primordial dimension of the *unus mundus*. It cannot be spatially located anywhere. To use Pribram's analogy, one cannot find consciousness by dissecting the brain or by viewing neural processes using such imaging techniques as fMRI scanning, anymore than one can find gravity by digging into the earth (2004, 11).

The illusion created by Dawkins is that God is a delusion because that which his concept of God denotes can not be found in the material universe of classical physics nor is such an external entity necessary to understanding the material bodies of which the cosmos is composed, including our own. The persistence of Dawkins's illusion is a by-product of something once necessary for the evolution of science: the underlying epistemology of classical physics and reductionist materialism in which both the mind of the observer and its role in scientific experimentation could be ignored or treated as an embarrassing artifact.

Historically, spirit had to be banished or driven from matter in order for the scientific understanding of the laws of the material universe to move beyond its beginnings and away from potential contamination by theology. As Schrödinger (1992) noted with characteristic irony, no personal God could be discovered in a universe from which anything personal, including the mind of the human observer, had been ousted by a priori definition of the subject matter permissible in science.

However, Einstein's prediction that the science that turned humanity away from God would one day return humanity to God began to be fulfilled when the existence and role of mind could no longer be overlooked or treated as epiphenomenal. The existence of rudimentary mindlike qualities at the quantum level of the implicate order and/or archetypal dimensions of mind coextensive with the universe restores mind to its rightful place in a science in which the existence and significance of the "personal equation" of the human observer must be accounted for.

The personal equation of the human observer is the psyche with a consciousness that has evolved to reflect the universe back to itself in the form of mathematically formulated laws on the quantum as well as the classical levels and to which the epiphanies of mathematical, scientific, and artistic inspiration are revealed. Penrose (2004, 1033) has expressed the view that a complete physics must account for the mentality of the observer. Before continuing with an elaborate case for God, however, I must counter some potential difficulties with simplistic tendencies to identify God with humanity, even in its collective form. This means exploring distinctions between the usage of the term *God* in the remainder of this book from such forms of ego-transcending collectivization as Marxism and variants of secular humanism in which the species as a whole is considered to be transcendent without being related to anything numinous or spiritual. Collectivization is antithetical to the Jungian individuation process, and dialectical materialism precludes religious freedom. Such twentieth-century existentialist definitions of God as "ultimate concern" (Paul Tillich) or the "ground of all being," while stripped of anthropomorphism, suffer from the deficiencies of being both philosophically vague and tenuous with respect to numinous significance and empirical foundation.

Collectivization: The God of Insects

As Teilhard de Chardin noted in *The Future of Man* (1964), mere collectivization as envisioned in such secular systems of thought as that of Karl Marx, with its overarching notions of dialectical materialism and dictatorship of the proletariat, resulted in forms of centralist social organization that became themselves the opium of the masses from which the people were supposed to be liberated. The hierarchical organization of societies remained, except that monarchies were replaced by commissars and dictators like Joseph Stalin and Chairman Mao. The narcotic of religion underwent a metamorphosis into mindless conformity to political doctrine and quasi-religious devotion to leaders who were virtually deified as archetypal heroes and saviors of their people. With the death of God, everything was permissible, including the mass murder of millions of people.

Needless to say perhaps, the egalitarian ideals of the revolution were buried beneath pressures to suppress individualism, dissent, and the apostasy of revisionism. Dissent was dangerous even in science, and as Kalervo Laurikainen (1988, 58) pointed out, political pressure was placed upon Niels Bohr to revise his views on the role of the observer's consciousness in the Copenhagen interpretation of quantum theory so that the Soviets could sit comfortably with their dialectical materialism. The role of the mind of the observer in this interpretation was considered to be particularly offensive to Soviet physicists. While atheism was the official party line, barely disguised religious sentiments were directed toward the state in lieu of ecclesiastical institutions. Thus God was repressed into the unconscious only to return in the guise of idolatry of the state and its dictators. I refer to this manifestation of repressed spirit and numinosity as the God of insects. As is the case in colonies of insects, such as beehives, in which no individuality exists, in totalitarian states the individuation process is repressed so that personal self-identity is subsumed to a mindless devotion to the state and its secular atheistic leaders, a point which I develop further in chapter 5.

Secular humanism, as a philosophical framework, adopted an overtly intellectual agnostic position on the existence of God, evolving during the Enlightenment period and embracing the ethos of empirical science. This was the philosophical position of eminent biologist Julian Huxley. Huxley described human beings as the "business managers" of evolution with a correspondingly awesome responsibility for the future of both the biosphere and the noosphere.

The problem with secular humanism is that it can result in an apotheosis of science into scientism with its own dogmas and doctrines that become obstacles to independence of mind and discovery as well as Kuhnian paradigm shifts. Indoctrination is not confined to conservative and fundamentalist religion, which can thwart or corrupt science; it can occur in the name of science in ways that are inimical to the Enlightenment and liberal ideals of secular humanism and scientific empiricism. The more profound difficulty, however, is with the underlying epistemology of a reductionist, metaphysical materialism, which, as I have argued, is of dubious tenability in a post–quantum mechanical science that has integrated mind into its explanatory domain. The metaphysical materialism of writers such as Dawkins is a doctrine about nature rather than an explanation of nature, as his tendency to substitute natural selection for God amply attests. But who is to say that natural selection in its extended use by Dawkins to apply to cosmology as well as the evolution of species is not also a God of figurative bees (devoid of individual psyches, personalities, and reflective consciousness) whose individuality is subsumed to the needs of the colony for whom the term *natural selection* is a form of collective quasi-religious mantra?

The Religion of Metaphysical Materialism

It is perhaps a supreme irony that the philosophical doctrine of metaphysical materialism has itself become quasi-religious in nature. It is expressed in thinly disguised form in the maxim, "greed is good," used by certain televangelists to provide a religious justification for conspicuous consumerism and for the consumption, as if by divine right, of the world's energy resources, including fossil fuels, by the few at the expense of the many. The consensus of science is that burning these fuels is the primary cause of global warming, which if left unchecked will result in a disaster of apocalyptic proportions for future generations. The perverse theology is that the acquisition of wealth and material possessions is a sign of being favored by God to the point that the human relationship to mammon becomes a numinous one.

Even if no explicit allusion is made to such a Calvinist concept of God, human beings are nevertheless indoctrinated, via the media and Internet, into believing that material goods will bring salvation in the form of transformation of their individual lives from the experience of emptiness and worthlessness to one of fullness and rapture. Indeed, the indoctrination is in the apparently secular form of attaching a supreme value to material products and the consumption of them, irrespective of the impact on humanity as a whole or the planet. But this quasi-religious transformation at the collective level is an alarmingly negative one, as the phenomenon of global warming and the financial crises throughout the Western world amply demonstrate.

Just as mindless devotion to the state and its leaders was characteristic of Marxism, so also the cult of consumerism demands acceptance of the market forces of economic rationalism both as articles of faith and as transcendent values in capitalist societies (see chapter 5). Market forces become the cultural equivalent of natural selection, polarizing and separating the haves from the have nots and, in their more covert theological form, the saved from the predestined damned. While Dawkins dismisses an anthropomorphic notion of God as a delusion, he seems to be unaware of the potentially transcendent and numinous forms assumed by materialism itself in economic rationalist doctrine as well as consumerism. Furthermore, Dawkins and his fellow skeptics fail to see the religious devotion of the compulsive gambler or the stock market investor, both of whom seek transformation of their lives through behavior that is no less ritualistic and dedicated than that of the theists who are subject to such derision by them.

Wars conducted in the name of God, which Dawkins regards as particularly damning of the world's religions, often turn out, on closer scrutiny, to be as much about coveting energy resources and territory as attempts to convert other nations to particular theologies. In other words, religion is used as a rationalization, but the real agenda concerns energy supplies such as oil. Examples of this would be the two Gulf Wars in the Middle East, and the First and Second World Wars could also be construed as being motivated in significant measure by competition for territory and resources irrespective of the ideologies used to justify them. In such conflicts the other is demonized and dehumanized on the basis of shadow projections. The secular religion of metaphysical materialism with its denial of mind and of the personhood of other human beings enables mass murder of civilians and policies such as extraordinary rendition to be implemented in a state of dissociation from feelings of empathy and remorse.

In short, conscience is corrupted by materialist doctrine and the depersonalization of others so that almost anything becomes permissible, including the use of tactical nuclear weapons. Materialism, in the third millennium, is a far greater menace than religious orthodoxy ever was, and a far greater menace than an evolving theology of the earth, because in the name of materialism, the planet and its resources exist simply to be exploited. A third millennium theology would encourage a global consciousness and holism or interconnectedness of all and a sense of the sacredness of the earth and of all life. It would also be universal rather than tribal.

Toward a Scientifically Informed Theology

A theology of the third millennium would be one which has begun to explore scientifically the foundations of the human experience of the numinous from the perspective of such disciplines as depth psychology and neuroscience. Such exploration, of course, is not new as, for example, the classic work of psychologist William James in the nineteenth century would attest. The post-Freudian psychoanalytic literature on the origins of religious experience is extensive, and quite recently a field has emerged that is referred to as neurotheology, dedicated to identifying the supposed neural substrate of religious experience, which in turn is assumed to be genetically encoded or programmed into relevant brain structure.

These sorts of enquiries generally do not begin with the assumption that either God or religious experience is necessarily delusional in nature, although the reductionist fallacy remains an omnipresent possibility in the form of the temptation to identify such phenomenology with brain processes. Skeptics like Dawkins, on the other hand, begin with the notion that God is a delusion as axiomatic or a synthetic a priori (factually true) assumption, rather than approaching the phenomena of religious experience as a subject for open-minded empirical enquiry and as revealing something of the nature of an evolving humanity to itself.

Dawkins's critique views religious experience and theism as, at best, by-products of something that once had evolutionary value and, at worst, as indistinguishable from the delusions and hallucinatory phenomena of florid psychosis. The possibility that humanity collectively is naturally religious and that the experience of the numinous as well as the search for meaning and self-transcendence is intrinsic to our evolutionary programming seems to be eclipsed by rationalist and materialist prejudice. This prejudice ignores the possibility that the image of God has an evolutionary history and evolves with humanity that, as Bohm (2002, 386) has suggested, has become the mirror in which the universe reflects upon itself. Skeptics like Dawkins are immobilists in the sense that they cannot grasp the symbolic transformations that the human experience and image of God have undergone since prehistoric times in the process of cultural evolution.

This cultural evolution of God is manifest in the numinous qualities once experienced in animistic nature gods and spirits represented in the cave paintings of the Neanderthals, in such anthropomorphic visions as that of the biblical genesis depicted in Michelangelo's Sistine Chapel frescoes, and culminating in such theological ideas as those of Teilhard de Chardin, Hans Küng, and Bede Griffiths (1989) as well as Wolfgang Pauli and David Bohm. It is as intellectually slothful to argue that God is a delusion on the basis of prescientific and archaic theological attempts to explain the numinous as it would be to attempt to limit the history and philosophy of science to the study of pre-Copernican theories of cosmology and the status of scientific knowledge in the medieval and pre-Enlightenment periods. The *imago Dei* or image of God evolves both phylogenetically and ontogenetically, a theme which I develop fully in chapter 6.

A theology of the third millennium would be one that encompasses, among other disciplines, depth psychology, quantum physics, and neuroscience. Sophisticated theologians have embraced the scientific revolutions that have occurred in astronomy, physics, and biology, including perhaps especially the theory of evolution. Such a theology, as Hans Küng writes in his latest work, *The Beginning of All Things: Science and Religion* (2007), is already one in which the schism between science and religion is being overcome through dialogue. However, it is also a theology that is not static but evolving with human consciousness and no longer rooted in primitive projection of human attributes onto the external universe. Rather, such a theology is one that acknowledges the cosmos within humanity, of which C. G. Jung was a pioneer.

Dawkins and his skeptical colleagues do not address a theology that is itself evolving while integrating the scientific revolutions that have occurred since the seventeenth century. Thus, Dawkins's critique and his notion of the God delusion, which he believes the collective psyche of humanity is suffering from, in reality addresses a theology that has been dying since the early twentieth century, except perhaps for the phenomenon of religious fundamentalism. It is easy to figuratively resurrect a system or species of thought destined for extinction with the sole purpose of ritually debunking and slaying it, as I believe Dawkins does with his God delusion. Paradoxically perhaps, the dreaming of indigenous peoples is conserved as precious precisely because of the insight it provides into the zeitgeist and mythology characteristic of the early phylogenetic history of humanity, as both cultural anthropologists and depth psychologists would attest.

Religious fundamentalism and scriptural literalism, whether Western or Eastern, are vulnerable to Dawkins's criticism, but these are relics of the theological infancy of humankind, while remaining fixed in such outmoded cosmologies as the static, pre-Copernican universe. By contrast, a theology of the third millennium would leave fundamentalist stories about God and creation myths such as that depicted in the book of Genesis behind, like the fairy tales, animistic thinking, and projections of childhood that populate the world with demons and monsters. The problem is not with myths as expressions of archetypes but with the literal interpretation of them as historic or empirical truths. George Bush's axis of evil was manifestly an archetypal projection of shadow qualities of this type. What is terrifying is that such projections can result in mass murder or the use of thermonuclear weapons. It is the anthropomorphic God of religious fundamentalism, (in which the archetype is clothed in patriarchal parental garments), which could be considered a delusion as Dawkins claims.

The concept of God espoused by Thomas Aquinas as the *prima causa* (first cause) has been dead since Newton formulated his classical laws and dispensed with any need for a deity to set the clockwork universe in motion. If there are archetypal dimensions of the Self, including the God image, that transcend spacetime as well as being implicit in the evolutionary process, such a temporally bound concept of an external God as the beginning of all things strips the archetype of its timeless or eternal quality.

A numinous dimension is implicit in the process of evolution as a cosmic ordering and regulating principle so that God becomes conscious and is completed by humankind in an awakening into the awesome reality of the supernaturalness of humanity. The archetypes as timeless cosmic ordering and regulating principles in evolution are in themselves numinous and consistent with a process or incarnational theology illuminated by depth psychology.

Depth psychology is one of the profound sources of inspiration for a theology of the third millennium. I shall argue that theology cannot be construed as merely an accidental by-product or the "misfiring of something useful" in terms of evolutionary survival, as Dawkins, for example, suggests with his example of the displacement of the experience of falling in love onto religious figures or symbolic representations. Rather than being epiphenomenal in this sense, I shall argue for the proposition that theology and the experience of the numinous is integral to the evolution of humanity itself and especially of mind and consciousness.

God is not only evolving through humanity, but also transhistorical, transcultural, transpersonal, and, in Jung's original sense, archetypal—timeless and eternal. However, conceived in this way, God is a reality that transcends the finite, spatiotemporally bound doctrines that have become theological systems of thought. The theology of the future will be less prone to containing God or the experience of the numinous in doctrinal formulations and become perhaps more mystical in its nature.

Theology and Depth Psychology

C. G. Jung, in *Modern Man in Search of a Soul* (1933), wrote of how the images and symbols of Christianity were losing their meaning so that people were no longer feeling "redeemed" and were turning to psychotherapists rather than the clergy. He therefore explored the transformational and numinous symbols that he referred to as the archetypes of the collective unconscious, including that of God. Jung, in his humility and scrupulous adherence to the attitude of empirical science, avoided attributing any necessary metaphysical significance to his discoveries, not even to the numinous symbols that became the subjects of his investigations. Yet he expressed the hope that his work would help redeem the symbols and myths of Christianity for the benefit of humankind. In that sense, he regarded Christianity as a figurative patient, which might be resurrected or transformed through his analytic treatment. Such archetypes as those of the death and rebirth of the Self were expressed in such transformational rituals as that of the mass about which Jung wrote an essay (Jung 1954).

In other words, Jung, as well as the depth psychologists like Michael Fordham and Rosemary Gordon who followed him, believed that theology could be enriched and greatly enlivened by raising the transformational and healing symbols of the collective unconscious into the light of consciousness. Fordham (1985), for instance, wrote an entire book chapter on the mysticism of St. John of the Cross, referring to the saint as the medieval equivalent and forerunner of a Jungian analyst while commenting on the implications of Jung's essays on Job and the Catholic mass for the contemporary understanding of the theological doctrine of the incarnation of God in humanity.

Dawkins's crude dismissal of mystical visions as being due to a "virus of the mind" or a mere derivative of sexual love fails to grasp the meaning of archetypal symbols and the emotional energy invested in them. As for libido, he appears to be unfamiliar with the Freudian notion of sublimation as well as Jung's extended understanding of that term as denoting psychic energy, including the numinous quality associated with the God archetype. By plunging into crass literalism instead of grasping the metaphors and symbols, Dawkins replicates the kind of error for which he despises religious fundamentalists. Perhaps he would interpret the "divine lover," referred to in the poetic utterances of St. John of the Cross, as disguised (not sublimated) homosexuality. What does Dawkins make of such magnificent structures as the cathedrals of Europe, erected during the Middle Ages, with spires soaring "heavenward"? Are these edifices to be construed as mere "spin-offs" of a once-useful phallocentric or homoerotic penis worship? Dawkin's crusade in *The God Delusion* is nothing less than the derision and deconstruction of the supernatural, external, interventionist, and anthropomorphic God of religious fundamentalism and of the three Abrahamic faiths (2006, 20). However, this concept is not to be conflated with the numinous Jungian God archetype implicit in nature or with the metaphysical aspects of Pauli's U-field, discussed in chapters

2 and 3. Furthermore, humanity does need to recover the unconscious archetypal foundations of symbols that have lost their original, mythic, redeeming, synthetic (Self-integrating), and numinous meanings and a capacity for authentic mystical experience. A quote from Jung's *Symbols of Transformation* enhances our understanding of the God archetype:

> Religious regression makes use of the parental imago, but only as a symbol—that is to say, it clothes the archetype in the image of the parents, just as it bodies forth the archetype's energy by making use of sensuous ideas like fire, light, heat, fecundity, generative power, and so on. In mysticism the inwardly perceived vision of the Divine is often nothing but sun or light and is rarely if ever personified. (1952b, 90)

Jung then illustrates this experience with an account of one of the visions of Hildegard of Bingen (1100–1178), who described "a living light... which is brighter far than the cloud which supports the sun" (ibid., 91). In such passages it is clear that the God archetype is a reality that transcends humanity, although human beings participate in it, for instance, in mystical experiences of the numinous. In chapter 3, I referred to the notion shared by Jung and Pauli that "archetypes are expressions of a cosmic order which is verifiable both in our observations of the external world and in the structure of the internal world of our psyche" (in Laurikainen 1988, 149).

Archetypal Symbols of the Numinous

One archetype that Jung considered to be of particular importance (as did Pauli) was the so-called *coniunctio oppositorum* or union of opposites, explored in *Psychology and Religion: West and East* (*Collected Works of C. G. Jung*, vol. 11) and *Symbols of Transformation* (vol. 5). Pauli saw in this archetype an expression of Bohr's complementarity principle, for example, with regard to the relationships between matter and spirit as well as the living and the nonliving. For Jung, the archetype was manifest in such symbols of inner wholeness and self-integration as the mandalas that appeared in the dreams of his patients and in such religious images as the eight-spoked wheel of Buddhism and the rose windows in Gothic cathedrals such as Chartres and Notre Dame in France. These external symbols corresponded to the internal phenomenological state of order, harmony, balance, and the rapture associated with mystical experiences.

Cultural, artistic expressions and structures reveal a connection between depth psychology and theology. For example, a correspondence could be demonstrated between the sun worship of ancient civilizations, such as Egypt and the Aztecs, and the sun as an archetypal symbol of the numinous. The sun symbol is present in Christianity as the halo surrounding the heads of Christ and canonized saints and in the monstrance used in the Catholic tradition to contain the Eucharist. (One might speculate as to whether some of the resistance to the Copernican theory in astronomy by Renaissance theologians might have sprung from an unconscious investment in the sun as a God representation.)

It is not difficult to think of the theologies of East and West as arid and archaic systems of religious thought, meaningless in the third millennium epoch of empirical science and technology in which God is a delusional relic of humankind's evolutionary and prescientific past. In an era of metaphysical materialism, according to skeptics like Dawkins, spirit has been banished from science and from the collective consciousness of humankind as it was in the seventeenth century by Newtonian (now classical) physics which exorcised God from the universe. This, incidentally, would mean that the exploration of Eastern mysticism for insights into mind by physicists as eminent as Schrödinger and Bohm have been aberrations about which scientists should be silent.

In chapter 1 I referred to the "revenge of spirit" which Pauli warned us about as being the inevitable result of psychic repression. This theme is further developed by the argument that materialism, devoid of animation from within by mind, is itself a delusion, albeit one about which Western civilization tends to be alarmingly blind and complacent, in spite of the demonstrated power of the atomic bomb unleashed on Hiroshima and the more recent phenomenon of global terrorism. In a rather grotesque way, mind as artificial intelligence is being imputed by some cognitive scientists to present-day computers, rather a stretch of the imagination, given the nonalgorithmic and noncomputable aspects of mentality described, for example, by Penrose.

As Paul Davies has commented, many notable scientists, including "Einstein, Pauli, Schrödinger, Heisenberg, Eddington, and Jeans have espoused mysticism" (1992, 226–227), referring to human beings as "animated stardust" (ibid., 232). However, as the aspirations of humankind have resulted in the creation of a global village as well as a noosphere, the question is whether the desire for transcendence through connection with something infinite or greater than oneself can be satisfied by a pursuit other than the exploration of outer (external) space. I have already mentioned how the pervasive narcissism and grandiosity of certain political leaders eclipses any possibility of experiencing the numinous or a transcendent dimension of being and a selfless participation in it. This search for transcendence has been traditionally a question addressed by theological systems that are encoded not only in thought or doctrine, but also in cultural and archetypal symbols, including those expressed in personal and collective myths, architecture, music, and science.

Before turning to the problems posed by Internet addiction, omnipresent computers, multinational corporations, and the future of humanity, I shall consider an example from the past which illustrates theological information as well as the archetypal symbolism and energy encrypted in it. The example is the Gothic cathedral of the medieval period with its soaring aspiration to touch the divine. The building of cathedrals was an act of devotion and of connection with God for those who erected them.

I referred earlier to Pribram's notion that the idea or concept and symbolic meaning of a cathedral cannot be inferred merely from the stones of which it is constructed. In fact, cathedrals such as Chartres, Notre Dame, Cologne, and Salisbury are sublime symbols, erected in stone, of humankind's inner aspiration for connection with something infinite, numinous, or transcending of the confines of the finite and mortal ego. Such structures, sometimes described as music frozen in stone, are still capable of awakening powerful feelings of awe and rapture in the twenty-first century, whether viewed from the outside or from within as examples of the *temenos* or sacred space in which the numinous and "real Presence" is contained and worshipped.

Thus, the great cathedrals are external representations of an archetypal reality within the collective unconscious of humankind, as well as being statements of theology carved and encoded in stone; they emphasized an upward and forward movement toward God who was thought, due to projection, to exist in the "heavens." It may seem to be remarkable, given the advances of science, that the universal and eternal human longing for the *unio mystica*, or union with the transcendent, can still be evoked by structures from bygone times in spite of the revolutions that have occurred in cosmology. This is what manifests their intrapsychic (internal) archetypal origins as well as the myth and theology encoded in them and given that Hiley and Pylkkänen describe the derivation of the English word *information* as "form put into process" (2005, 19).

When viewing the construction of skyscrapers today, devoted to the pursuit of consumerism and the exploitation of the earth, while often throwing the cathedrals into shadow, it is difficult to imagine the mysticism expressed in the work expended to erect the cavernous cathedrals whose stained glass and intricate carvings, as well as the inner space itself, were creative inspirations of the divine fire stolen from the gods in the myth of Prometheus (the same symbolic fire that breathes life into the equations of physics for scientists like Schrödinger, Hawking, and Penrose).

The theology encoded in modern towers of glass and steel is that of metaphysical materialism in its economic expression. Rather than connecting with something numinous, ego-transcending, and Other-centered, the soaring "religious" aspiration is that of acquiring boundless money and power such that the reward of triumphing over fate or on the stock exchange inflates the ego with godlike feelings of omnipotence and grandeur. This state is one of downward transcendence and may involve the ruthless exploitation of other people and of the earth's resources. The underlying myth resembles that of Icarus, whose hubris led him to fly too close to the sun so that his wax wings melted and he crashed headlong to the earth.

The Future: Reintegrating Science and Religion

One of the unintended consequences of the schism between science and religion which began in the seventeenth century was the banishment of mind and spirit from science. This not only left science without an explanation of the role and significance of the human observer whose psyche nevertheless created scientific theories, it also resulted in the demotion of myth and theology to the status of primitive and prescientific attempts to understand the universe. No personal God could be found in a space and time from which anything personal had been excluded. That both mythology and theology could be construed as epiphanies of the cosmic ordering and regulating principles (archetypes) underlying the regularities and laws to be observed in both the external and internal phenomenal worlds remained largely unconscious, at least until the role of the observer and mind, in its conscious and unconscious aspects, could no longer be ignored with the quantum revolution in physics and the overthrow of rationalism by depth psychology in the early twentieth century.

Both of these revolutions, I shall argue, have played a role in laying the foundation for a reintegration of science and theology, both of which confront dimensions of reality that are neither purely rational nor bound by space and time as was the classical physics of Newton and the psychology of Skinner, which had no place for the mental. Such notions represented such an affront to the dominance of reason, which had been established as an axiom of science, that even Einstein never entirely surrendered his investment in classical physics or his belief that the paradoxes of quantum theory would eventually be resolved within a theoretical framework in which the reign of the old causality was restored. Dawkins openly acknowledges the relative poverty of his knowledge of psychology, and his treatment of quantum physics, particularly his discussion of the Copenhagen interpretation and of Schrödinger's cat as a parody of it, seems to be grossly misleading. However, by no mere coincidence perhaps, it is from the fields of depth psychology and quantum physics especially that the most salient challenge to his notion of God being a delusion can be mounted.

Both of these disciplines, as Laurikainen (1988) has pointed out, address influences that are independent of space and time as well as the role of mind and reflective consciousness as emergent evolutionary properties. From quantum physics has arisen the notion that the mental and the physical aspects of reality stand in a relationship of complementarity to one another and that it is not possible to separate the observer from what he sees. The interaction of the observer and the quantum system had become such that in the Copenhagen interpretation of Bohr and Pauli and in the view of Heisenberg in formulating the uncertainty principle, classical detachment is not possible. (Indeed, the quantum theory itself is a product of mind.) Pauli wrote of such relationships as being characterized by an indivisible wholeness as well as expressing the archetype of the union of opposites. When Pauli referred to the archetypes as cosmic ordering and regulating principles he was discussing factors that were both timeless and unconscious determinants of the patterns and mathematical laws to be discovered in the internal and external worlds.

Similarly, Bohm in his elucidation of the implicate order, was referring to a Mind extending beyond that of the human species and coextensive with the universe itself, where active information provided the link or bridge between mind and matter, even at the quantum level and prior to the emergence of consciousness. Quantum information theory and computing, which may have been discovered already by biosystems, can be construed as monumental extensions of Bohm's bridge. In Pauli's language, cosmic ordering principles, which are timeless or eternal and corrigible to mathematical formulation by human beings and which have a mental as well as a physical aspect are already transcendent in nature.

The notion of participation in nature as well as creating nature has not simply changed the role of the observer in science. It has revealed, through quantum physicists themselves, something extraordinary about the nature of the observer and of mind and consciousness in reflecting, creating, and acting upon the universe, rather than being evolved by nature, passively adapting to the environment, as Dawkins and others of like mind believe. Being, as Bohm wrote, the "mirror created by the universe to reflect upon itself" is not only an active role, it is also a supremely transcendent one (2002, 389).

Partaking of and participating in a transcendent order, which includes the notion of infinite Mind, is another way of experiencing the creation of a theology through the creativity of science itself and as a source of positively rapturous connection with something numinous. This is a far different idea than Dawkins's notion of God as a mere spin-off of something once useful. The acts of creation referred to not only reveal the divinity immanent within humanity, they also demonstrate the absurdity and delusional nature of the belief that chance and natural selection are a sufficient explanation of the observer whose role is to reflect the universe to itself. Paradoxically, if humanity has evolved by chance, there is nevertheless a sublime purpose to its existence, part of which is to explain the wisdom and lawfulness of the universe, a reality captured metaphorically in Michelangelo's fresco in the Sistine Chapel. A science that engages in cognitive repression of the meaning of the observer is one destined to remain eternally incomplete.

Perhaps the new myth for humanity is the undoing of such repression and of mediating between the conscious and the unconscious aspects of being, as does a modern psychoanalyst. Science is perhaps becoming the medium through which the new "prophets," as archetypal messengers of God, communicate the mystery and meaning of the cosmos to humanity. Through the heightened consciousness of the observer, there also occurs an awakening of God. In the process of establishing a case for the possibility of reintegrating science and theology, I simply note in passing that this enterprise has been underway since at least the middle of the twentieth century, and I have yet to deal with the voluminous contributions from depth psychology.

God on the Couch: Revelations from Depth Psychology

Cognitive psychology, because its underlying epistemology is still that of classical physics and due to its tendency to overvalue rationalism, has little to offer in the attempt to create bridges between science and theology. Its project is thoroughly materialist in spite of lip service in recent years to the importance of the search for meaning and spirituality. And although cognitive behavioral therapy has imported the concept of the unconscious from psychoanalysis, it has not adequately liberated the notion from being spatiotemporally bound rather than timeless and identified with brain processes. Thus, the contributions of such depth psychologists as Jung and even Freud are either viewed with suspicion or consigned to a theoretical limbo as pseudoscientific. It is perhaps significant, in this meaningful connection, that the quantum physicists to whom I have referred have turned to depth psychology, rather than the new "mindfulness" of cognitive behavioral therapy, in attempting to understand the role of the observer.

In depth psychology Jung, having collaborated with Pauli, used the term *personal equation* to refer to the interaction between the observer's psyche and quantum phenomena. He perceived an analogy between this situation and that which evolved between the analyst and patient in the transference/countertransference nexus of psychotherapy. Jung used the analogy of alchemical transformation to refer to this situation with the clear implication that both the analyst and the patient are actively involved in the transformative process and changed by it. Before proceeding further with an elucidation of the experience of God from the perspective of the analyst's couch, I shall make a brief detour into thesis eight of the Copenhagen interpretation of quantum physics concerning the mind of the observer.

This thesis is outlined by Laurikainen (1988) in his book on the philosophical thought of Wolfgang Pauli. In essence, the notion is that observation is always the result of interplay between the consciousness of the observer and the external world, where the measuring apparatus of the experimenter is considered to be an extension of the sense organs of the observer. Thus the observer is not merely a spectator but also an actor who is creating nature and whose theories are the result of a great deal of preparatory work in the unconscious. Without psyche, as Jung argued, there would be no theory. However, theories are formal statements of those patterns and regularities which emerge into consciousness as epiphanies of the archetypal cosmic ordering and regulating principles, in the form of mathematical and scientific insights like those described by Penrose as nonalgorithmic and noncomputable.

What is not frequently acknowledged is the correspondence between theoretical insights ostensibly about the external cosmos and processes within the phenomenal internal world of the psyche, especially in its unconscious aspect. The reality of the psyche is neither spatiotemporally bound nor identifiable with matter, not even that of the brain, in any crude reductionist manner. The intellectual cloud of fog that has surrounded the mind/matter or psychophysical problem since Descartes is dispelled considerably if this correspondence is understood as itself an expression of the complementarity principle as a mode of perceiving the relationship between mind and matter. This may make more sense of Pribram's remark to Eugene Wigner that perhaps "quantum physics is really psychology" (2004, 13). Again, as Pribram has pointed out, "it is a psychological process, mathematics, that describes the relationships organizing matter so that physics is rooted in both matter and mind" (2004, 14).

Returning to what the exploration of the unconscious reveals about the experience of the numinous (or God) in such archetypal forms as myth and transformational symbols, the energy and power of living myths and the archetypal symbols of the collective unconscious are to be discovered in the great religions of both East and West and in the dreams of human beings searching for an experience of the numinous on the analytical couch. The dominant myth in Western civilization is that the god of metaphysical materialism will deliver humankind from the ravages of poverty and the scourge of disease, thereby resulting in the redemption of wealth, with an abundance of things and an "immortality" in this life amounting to an indefinite postponement of physical death. However, this could be viewed as another manifestation of the archetype of the *puer aeternus* or eternal child with its perpetual narcissism and refusal to rise to the challenges and responsibility of adulthood and the future of humanity alike.

In *Modern Man in Search of a Soul* (1933), Jung noted that amongst his patients in the second half of life, there had not been one whose neurosis did not require the restoration of a religious attitude for a lasting "cure," restoration or transformation of the Self, to be accomplished. In the dreams of his patients, many of whom today would be diagnosed as suffering from narcissistic or borderline personality disorders, Jung discovered intimations of the numinous from the unconscious in the form of mandala symbols of wholeness and Self-integration as well as the archetypal themes of death and rebirth.

It might be wise to note here that to Jung, the Self was both the central organizing principle and totality of the personality, with unconscious dimensions that were timeless and hence not spatiotemporally bound. The patients of Jung and his followers, as well as those of psychoanalysts and Self psychologist Heinz Kohut, were seeking the restoration of a revivified and positive sense of self-identity as well as the awakening of a sense of meaning and transpersonal purpose in life rather than either restructured thoughts or behavior modification as short-term solutions.

Contemporary human beings, in other words, were turning to psychotherapists for the experience of inner transformation and connection with something numinous and transcendent. Such experiences had historically been sought within religious systems, but many people were no longer able to feel "redeemed" or to find an inner correspondence and resonance with the external symbols and rituals, especially those codified in Christianity.

Conversely, connecting with the unconscious and archetypal roots of numinous experience could enable some patients to recover the symbolic meaning of such ritual dramas as the mass and to discover, as one Buddhist monk noted, the extraordinary, transformative significance of the Eucharist, that of partaking in and becoming one with God rather than blindly receiving a wafer with only a vague intellectual idea of the medieval doctrine of transubstantiation. An analogy might be the appreciation of a Shakespearean play by an Elizabethan audience compared with the experience by someone from a radically different culture. Jung himself, while avoiding metaphysical assertions, developed an analytical psychology which nevertheless provides a bridge that allows two-way traffic between theologians and psychologists.

Illusion Revisited

Sigmund Freud, as I pointed out in chapter 1, regarded religion as an illusion without a future, though he was able to respect and to collaborate with such religious persons as Lutheran pastor Oskar Pfister. While uncompromising in his view that scientific rationalism would relegate religious systems of thought to the status of relics of humankind's cultural evolutionary past, Freud was endowed with the humility to acknowledge that his own position may have been influenced by his background in mechanistic science. His hope seems to have been that psychoanalytic exploration of the mind, especially in its unconscious aspects, would replace an outmoded theological understanding of the human condition. To Freud, religions were really collective or shared delusional thought systems rooted in infantile wish fulfillment and denial of the finality of death. His position therefore had much in common with that of Richard Dawkins's notion of a God delusion and with those of such passionate skeptics as philosopher Bertrand Russell and psychologist Michael Shermer with regard to the issue of personal immortality or self-continuity beyond death.

Although some aspects of Freud's explanation of the origins of patriarchal religion, such as Oedipal guilt over the killing of an ancestral father by a primal horde of sons, remain as imaginative and as speculative as Dawkins's own convenient fictions about memes and the imaginary friend or Binker phenomenon in childhood. As Dawkins himself put it, "Gods and Binkers have in common the power to comfort" while being companions, protectors, and "sounding boards for trying out ideas" (2006, 349–352). And like an anthropomorphic God, a Binker can remain an immutable source of consolation throughout life, during the vicissitudes of personal growth and crisis. A Binker's existence need be no more subject to premature "reality testing" than an infant's teddy bear, which is as much created in fantasy as it is something given to the child by the mother as a source of comfort and reassurance in her unavoidable absences. Unlike the "good enough mother" described by psychoanalyst Donald Winnicott (1971), however, I suspect that

Dawkins would miss the vital creative and symbolic significance of teddy bears and Binkers alike. Perhaps he would tend as a zealous rationalist, to be critical of the infant's emerging capacity for the use of illusion in creating and participating in culture throughout life, a theme to which I shall now turn in considering religion.

Later developments in psychoanalysis, beginning with the work of Winnicott in *Playing and Reality* (1971), placed illusion on a different and more positive footing in the context of understanding the development of the infant's self and inner life of fantasy and creative imagination, in the relationship with its mother. Central to this framework was the notion of the so-called transitional object, which occupied a mental space between infant and mother. Objects such as teddy bears are both given to the infant and created by it on the basis of fantasy. Thus, the transitional object becomes the first symbol of the mother's calming and reassuring presence as well as being something that can be created and destroyed by the infant in its play. The illusion is allowed by the mother, whose absences thereby become tolerable rather than becoming catastrophic due to the threatened loss of the experience of being symbolically as well as emotionally sustained or held in being.

In the in-between space that the transitional object occupies, it becomes the focus of creative illusion and unconscious fantasy. Within the theoretical framework developed by Winnicott, illusion acquired a remarkably positive connotation as the imaginative and creative source of culture and religion. Even science, aside from its inspirational aspects in the form of new insights and connections, could be conceived as playing with ideas on the basis of the same curiosity with which the child questions and explores its world.

This world is originally the microcosm that it shares with the mother and represents the beginning of all things from the infant's perspective. Thus, illusion is not to be confused with pathological distortion of reality or delusional systems of belief as Freud originally proposed and Dawkins seems to believe. It is at work for instance, in watching an opera or play in which one is engaged by the illusion created by the drama and music while also knowing that the performers are playing characters within the frame of the artistic presentation instead of being themselves.

The Jesuit psychoanalyst William Meissner (1984) has applied Winnicott's notion of illusion to religion as an expression of culture.

Meissner regards the individual's "God representation" or image as a transitional phenomenon which, like the child's teddy bear, may be sustained throughout the life cycle or consigned to a limbo of nonimportance only to be resurrected at certain times. The God representation is given to the child by its family, culture, and faith tradition while undergoing various transformations with the evolution of the Self. It may be rebelliously rejected, sometimes to be picked up again, perhaps in the autumn of life or on the internal quest for meaning, purpose, and self-transcendence. The nature of religious transitional objects (like the crucifix or rosary) will, of course, be contingent upon the faith tradition of the individual.

Meissner writes, "If Freud wished to rule out illusion and to destroy it, Winnicott wishes to foster it and to increase man's capacity for creatively experiencing it.... It is through illusion that the human spirit is nourished.... The man without imagination, without the capacity for play or for creative illusion, is condemned to a sterile world without color or variety, without the continual enrichment of man's creative capacities" (1984, 177). With regard to the transitional objects and phenomena of religion Meissner writes, "The God-representation has a special place in that it is uniquely connected to man's sense of himself, of the meaning and purpose of his existence and his ultimate destiny" (ibid., 180). With regard to the symbols of religious belief systems, he comments that "in this category we can include the crucifix, the cross, the symbolic actions and gestures of the Roman Catholic Mass.... the Star of David, the menorah, and the prayers and rituals of liturgical practice.... They are religious symbols and as such become vehicles for the expression of meanings and values that transcend their physical characteristics" (ibid., 181).

Religious transitional objects are also created by the individual on the basis of unconscious fantasy and, although Meissner does not mention this possibility, archetypal projection. The rose windows in the great cathedrals of Europe could be construed as such projections, represented in stained glass and stone, of the archetypal symbol of wholeness, cosmic order, and harmony, also found in the mandalas produced by individuals undergoing analytically oriented psychotherapy.

Meissner emphasizes that, as with other imaginative cultural products such as great music and literature, religious illusions have become shared by significant groups of persons by a *consensus gentium* or general agreement. Those who insist too fervently upon the objective "truth" of their particular illusions tend to be regarded as delusional. Fundamentalists, for instance, have difficulty tolerating dissent from their literal interpretations of scriptures, which may seem absurd to "unbelievers" who do not share their illusions. Fundamentalists also seem to lack an evolved symbolic function and hence a grasp of the archetypal and mythological themes encoded in their holy books, while revealing cosmic truths about the numinosity of humanity to itself.

CHAPTER 5

Myth, Symbol, and Transformation

It is almost a truism that, in Western societies, once transformative myths and symbolic rituals have lost much of their meaning and dramatic impact. The Catholic mass, for instance, about which Jung wrote an extensive essay (1954), was once the external enactment of a transformational process within the collective psyche, involving the archetypes of death and rebirth. The mass was to be understood as a symbolic rite of inner transformation and spiritual renewal, whereby ego consciousness encountered a transcendent reality beyond its own finiteness. Shadow qualities had to be acknowledged in the form of a confession prior to communion with God, represented in Christ made present through the rite of transubstantiation in the Eucharist. To participate in the rite was to encounter the eternal in the present.

Jung's essay goes into more detail, but suffice it to say that what was once a drama played out within the soaring inner spaces of Gothic cathedrals, with correspondingly sublime and elevating music, has tended to degenerate into an empty ritual that is no longer vivifying for the Western soul. The external symbolic enactment no longer finds a resonance within the individual or collective psyche as the compelling expression of a contemporary myth of heroism and redemption from dark and sinister forces. Nor is the ritual drama of the mass necessarily an inner experiential encounter with the symbolic Christ as the archetypal savior and source of rebirth.

Jung's contribution, I believe, was to try to resurrect the lost meaning and vitality of the transformation symbolism and mythology encoded in the mass. Liturgical reforms and attempts to modernize the mass with popular music more suited to rock festivals than soaring cathedrals may have had the unintended consequence of destroying much of the mystery encrypted in the ritual drama, rather than making the symbols more accessible to a collective consciousness in which their meaning had been largely lost. This point was made by the poet T. S. Eliot, who apparently insisted that the passion play, like his own drama *Murder in the Cathedral*, be well performed. The quality of the performance of the liturgy in words, symbolic actions, and music might enhance the experience of archetypal motifs contained in the ritual drama as Dols has suggested. Elucidating this argument, Dols writes that "liturgy should contain more not less of traditional Catholic symbology with diminished reliance on liturgical revisions in contemporary language. The problem is not semantic but theological-psychological. The purpose of the liturgy is to convey, engage, and stir the mythic motifs that from the beginning have been at the heart of the ritual. Drama, music, silence, movement, art, dance, and imaginal meditation become valuable means to that end" (1987, 141).

The problem is that merely dressing up religious ceremonies such as the mass with popular rock music and changing the staging of both the drama and the actors does not necessarily bring the underlying archetypes to life in a way that engages the minds and hearts of twenty-first-century people. Changing the position of the altar and using vernacular language as well as rock music may tend to diminish the numinosity and mystery of the ritual. The archetypal symbol of Christ crucified between two thieves once conveyed both the pain of psychic dismemberment and the wholeness of reconciling the opposites of light and darkness, good and evil into a harmonious unity (the *coniunctio oppositorum*). Perhaps this is the reason that Jung referred to the mass as the rite of individuation. In "Transformation Symbolism in the Mass," Jung wrote that "the mystery of the Eucharist transforms the soul of the empirical man, who is only a part of himself, into his totality, symbolically expressed by Christ. In this sense, therefore, we can speak of the Mass as the rite of the individuation process" (1954, 273).

Similarly, the misguided attempt to demythologize religions, including Christianity, may have robbed these traditions of both the meaning and the emotional richness of their symbols, leaving only an absurd literalism in interpreting the myths as history or looking for archaeological evidence to verify scriptures that are in fact better understood as the historical conduits of archetypes which reveal human nature rather than change it. Such literalism and concretism betray the absence of an adequately evolved symbolic function or point to a symbolic function which has been lost such that the cultural and spiritual significance of the myths and the archetypes of which they are manifestations have become eclipsed from consciousness. Contemporary humanity is left as a result in a state of spiritual poverty and prone to an idolatrous devotion to technologies that have the power to destroy their creators.

Fundamentalism: The Real Delusions about God

I dealt briefly with religious fundamentalism in chapter 2; here I want to amplify the notion that its resurgence in the Abrahamic faiths especially is a potent source of very dangerous delusions about God, while providing agnostics and skeptics like Dawkins with copious ammunition to use against theism, at least in its more primitive forms. The clear and present danger is the use of scriptural literalism to rationalize wars against suitably demonized nations, wars that are in reality motivated by the collective shadow qualities in the Western psyche of greed and the aggressive desire to exploit the energy resources of the Middle East, especially oil.

The image of God used in the justification of such militant ventures belongs, as Bishop John Shelby Spong (1996) has observed, in the first century of Christianity when the events depicted in the apocalypse were interpreted as concrete predictions of an imminent second coming of the Messiah and the destruction of the known world. The fundamentalist representation of God retains its status as an anthropomorphic projection, one that is invested with humankind's own collective shadow qualities and destructiveness. The axis of evil, for instance, is as much a human construct as the anthropomorphic, interventionist image of God invoked to rationalize strikes against it.

The irony is that a very real apocalypse is now technologically possible, brought about not by divine intervention but by human beings in the name of a pre-Copernican, fundamentalist deity whose morality was as dubious as his personality was unstable and dark. As observed by Jung in his essay on Job (1952a), the Old Testament Yahweh exhibited attitudes of jealousy, wrathfulness, megalomania, and sadism toward his own creation, including humanity and his own son, represented in the mythic figure of Christ. A symbolic second coming and incarnation of Jung's dark side of God could perhaps be one interpretation of current world events, but this is not what the fundamentalists have in mind with their eschatological theologies and belief in biblical inerrancy.

The problem with religious fundamentalism, aside from its paranoia and suspicion about science, is that it interprets the scriptures as history, rather than as myth and moral allegory intended to illuminate the human condition, while clinging to a cosmology and a view of the origins of both life and humankind known to be false in empirical scientific terms. Unfortunately, this is characteristic of evangelical, Protestant, and ultraconservative Catholic Christianity alike. In the twenty-first century, such fundamentalism is a powerful impediment to humanity's search for meaning and for a living experience of a numinous or transcendent dimension of being. Similarly, the fundamentalist insistence on the inerrancy of scripture found in Judaism and Islam is just as potentially dangerous as that which has its historical roots in Christianity. The notion of biblical inerrancy, however, reveals the absurdity of comparisons of immobilist doctrines like creationism and intelligent design with empirical scientific theories. Scientific theories are defined by being both falsifiable and probabilistic rather than being dogmatically proclaimed as true.

One of the worst and most grandiose delusions about God promoted by religious fundamentalism is the righteous system of thought in which a singular human group perceives itself as the elect or chosen people. This delusion is not only dangerous and a menace to world peace, it constitutes a profound obstacle to interfaith dialogue and the perception of the interconnectedness and sacredness of all human beings, irrespective of faith tradition. It is an impediment to the discovery of the universal, archetypal, and eternal truths and to the continuing incarnation of God described by Jung that humankind's faith traditions have in common. In "Answer to Job," Jung wrote, "Only through the most extreme and menacing conflict does the Christian experience deliverance into divinity, always provided that he does not break, but accepts the burden of being marked out by God. In this way alone can the *imago Dei* realize itself in him and God become man" (1952a, 417).

Since the publication of Sigmund Freud's *The Interpretation of Dreams* in 1900, the symbolic meaning of dream content has been viewed as the *via regis* or royal road to the understanding of the unconscious in its personal and collective mythological aspects. This symbolic attitude, I have suggested, is precisely what is missing in fundamentalism so that the meaning of religious myths and archetypes is missed and lost. By coercively insisting upon literalism in interpreting scripture, fundamentalists actually destroy the potential power and redeeming value of humankind's great religions. The Abrahamic faith traditions are in desperate need of restoration and redemption if they are to facilitate an attitude of geopolitical holism and the evolution of a third millennium theology.

Such resurrection to meaning and new life, however, will not come from dressing up fundamentalist religion with sophisticated technologies and the latest musical fads. Such devices may be conducive to mass hypnosis of a type familiar from Hitler's Nuremberg rallies and to a descent into the mentality of the collective, which dissociated itself from the horrors of the holocaust and the mass murders of Stalin. But they cannot result in either an authentic experience of inner wholeness or mystical union with a transcendent or numinous reality. Genuine mystical experience enlivens the Self and awakens a compassion which embraces the earth. It is not a form of collective anesthesia of the mind or conformity to herd mentality. Perhaps the greatest casualty of all forms of fundamentalism, however, is truth as well as the reality testing and contact described by depth psychologists and encouraged by empirical science and its philosophy.

Fundamentalisms are humankind's collective delusions about God, masquerading in the shallow, narcissistic modernity of rock music with its technology and popular idols. The medium does not change the message even if it ensnares those who are vulnerable in nets of mind-numbingly loud music and lighting effects, known to be conducive to brainwashing and the acceptance of herd conformity. Susceptibility is attributable to adolescent identity confusion and the search for a sense of belonging to overcome social alienation, factors observed in such movements as the Hitler youth.

Skeptics, however, infer from the existence of fundamentalist delusions that all concepts of the numinous must be delusional. Before returning to contemporary understandings of religious experience from depth psychology, I shall outline some secular manifestations of the thinly veiled quest for numinous experience, which are also compelling examples of the apotheosis of materialism.

God in Secular Disguises

Sidney Blumenthal has written of the pervasive influence of religious conservatism upon the United States presidency and political policy entangled with these ideological factors. Blumenthal writes, "In 1980, Reagan anointed the religious right as ministers of the social issue. You can't endorse me but I endorse you.... The Reagan White House helped direct the takeover of the Southern Baptist Convention [SBC], radically altering its theological positions. The SBC had previously upheld the right of abortion and the strict separation of church and state. By 1982 all these tenets had been reversed" (2006, 164). Continuing his treatment of the entanglement between conservative theology and state affairs, he goes on to say that "in 2004, evangelical Protestant and conservative catholic bishops were crucial in mobilizing voters on Bush's behalf.... To the conservative Catholic bishops, Kerry represented their worst nightmare—a liberal Catholic as the most powerful man in the world—and they donned inquisitors' robes to issue maledictions that he should not receive communion" (ibid., 165).

Eroding the separation between church and state meant that the anointing of such secular leaders as presidents and prime ministers has begun to resemble the anointing once associated with the election of ecclesiastical elders, archbishops, or Renaissance popes. In truly democratic societies religious expression is neither repressed, as it is in materialist, totalitarian systems, nor is it allowed to create a de facto theocratic state with policies determined by ecclesiastical authorities and groups. The Constitution of the United States has enshrined freedom of religious expression as a fundamental and inalienable human right. However the blurring of boundaries between church and state that has occurred, for instance, under Ronald Reagan and George W. Bush, can facilitate the projection of mythic and quasi-numinous qualities onto secular leaders who then become symbolic heroes and savior figures for their people, who are held in a state of infantile regression by inducing fear of economic insecurity or suitably demonized enemies (otherwise known as terrorists, or, once upon a time, as communists).

Though disguised in secular form the myths evoked by political leaders involve much the same hagiography and demonology as those of historical epochs, with allusions to such dichotomies as good and evil, light and darkness, in the language of politics. Contemporary secular priests, prophets, messengers of the gods, and avenging angels descend to earth and destroy cities from aircraft or with weapons of mass destruction instead of the forces of nature misconstrued as acts of God on the basis of animistic projection. As always, the "dark side," as it is referred to in the Star Wars trilogy, belongs to demonized ethnic or religious groups against which the crusades are being waged just as they were in the Middle Ages, though now with much more devastation of civilian populations and biblical "massacre of innocents." With the benefit of historical hindsight it is not difficult to perceive the demonic myths and dark archetypal images constellated by Hitler and Stalin, while collective denial and blindness obscure such forces in contemporary political leaders of similar status. This is because, of course, contemporary political leaders represent the eternal and archetypal forces of light fighting against the darkness that has replaced the once evil "empire" of the Soviet Union.

Another example of numinosity disguised in secular form is the phenomenon of rock music with its cult figures such as Elvis Presley, who is venerated in death much as were saints in past centuries. As ecclesiastical institutions have gradually lost the once awesome power of their myths, symbols, and rituals to serve as conduits of archetypal energy, secular and collective movements have gradually taken their place. The expansive inner space of the cathedrals, in which the rites of transformation were enacted with exquisite beauty and sublime music to set the soul soaring, has been largely replaced by the outdoor spaces utilized by rock festivals during which pop idols for the masses are ritually created by the high priests and acolytes of narcissism and grandiosity of self. Of course, exceptional visionaries like Bob Dylan and Bono have contributed greatly to transforming collective consciousness while deliberately not cultivating the status of gods. Yet the unconscious hunger for transcendence and vivification of the spirit can be dumbed down and numbed through the administration of an opiate of mindless noise and meaningless meandering incantations.

The danger in a secular age in need of the restoration of an authentic sense of the numinous is that those upon whom archetypal images are projected will unknowingly become incarnations of them and succumb either to madness or the euphoria of substance abuse as a substitute for sacramental or transformative religious experience. This fate has befallen many prior to their twilight as secular idols.

Those religious institutions, including the Pentecostal churches, that succumb to the temptation to dress up their outmoded fundamentalist messages with secular music and bombardment of the senses do so in the deluded expectation that they are therefore mass-producing conversions to their doctrines, and hence, the experience of redemption with the promise of an eternity of rapture. In reality, they are in danger of creating an infantile dependency upon their elders, whose doctrines about the goodness of prosperity and greed are at variance with the beatitudes of the Sermon on the Mount, in which the poor are declared blessed and inheritors of the earth.

Secularism

Contemporary secularism, which is ostensibly value-free while nevertheless being rooted in an underlying doctrine, is a system of thought sometimes referred to as secular humanism. Secularism promotes a separation of church and state as well as a separation between church and the systems of education and higher learning. Independent schools and universities have been established in Western societies by various Christian churches in part at least because of the secularization of state-funded educational institutions in which religious studies have been ousted. However, democracy appropriately allows intellectual freedom for agnostics and atheists and those opposed to the teaching of religion. As a philosophical doctrine, secularism is usually associated with a humanistic frame of values and ethics that assiduously avoids reference to concepts of God or to anything of a numinous nature about either the human condition or the universe itself. The intention since the Enlightenment has been that of safeguarding intellectual freedom and protecting science from corruption by religious or political influences. However, this attempt to exorcise God from education and politics is largely illusory.

Instead of traditional theologies, the religion of materialism in its various guises becomes the invisible hand guiding both the state and institutions of learning, including universities. Secularism is a direct descendant of Enlightenment thinking, and though espousing tolerance, it can be militant in its opposition to religious ideologies while remaining oblivious to its foundations in metaphysical materialism. This militancy, espoused by skeptics like Richard Dawkins, is at times reminiscent of the zeal with which the Inquisition once attempted to root out heretical theological doctrines while insisting upon scriptural inerrancy. Dawkins is a devoutly religious atheist whose creed of dogmatic neo-Darwinism wants to eliminate religion altogether.

Thus, in secular university education concepts of the numinous have been ritually defined as meaningless in a positivist philosophy that regards religion as a prescientific system of thought, which a few lessons in the correct use of language can deconstruct or dispose of. Science could simply have nothing to say about the existence of a personal God, who has become a *Deus absconditus*, nowhere to be found in spacetime. On this point I shall quote Schrödinger directly: "No personal God can form part of a world model that has only become accessible at the cost of removing everything personal from it" (1992, 138). In classical physics, this exclusion extended to the personality and mind of the human observer as well as God. I shall have more to say about the articles of faith contained in agnosticism with its Enlightenment origins in the postscript.

The Religion of the State

When Karl Marx in his manifesto called upon the workers of all lands to unite he was introducing a secular religion of the state while regarding theism as the opiate of the people. Religion held human populations in a position of infantile dependency and fear of damnation. Thus, in Marxist thought compliance by the masses to theological doctrine and ecclesiastical authority was a condition for experiencing the opiate of redemption from the suffering of capitalist class oppression and the hopelessness of their perpetual poverty in an afterlife of heavenly reward and bliss. Marxist philosophy was referred to as dialectical materialism, and instead of the twin tyrannies of church and capitalist state, dictatorship of the proletariat would become the rule once the revolution was accomplished. Although it was militantly atheistic, Marxism evolved into a materialist theology of devotion to the state and its leaders, a thinly disguised religion with damnation for dissenters promised in the here and now in gulags and mental asylums rather than in some post-death existence.

Indeed, the charismatic leaders of various Marxist regimes became venerated as archetypal heroes and saviors of their people in ways that were remarkably reminiscent of such religious figures as the pope or the Dalai Lama. I would argue that the apparently universal human striving for connection with something numinous or infinite is not successfully repressed in totalitarian movements and political regimes.

Even when cathedrals are bombed, religious teaching forbidden, or such enlightened beings as the Dalai Lama are driven into exile by an oppressor masquerading as a liberator of the people, human beings remain naturally religious. However, while overt religious practice and ritual are driven underground, the numinous striving that remains, even on an unconscious level of the psyche, is projected onto the state. In contrast to Dawkins, I would argue that such resilience of the numinous factor suggests origins in an archetypal, cosmic ordering principle with evolutionary survival value for humanity. Consider some examples of totalitarian states operating as religious systems, in other words, situations in which a religion of the state rises from the ashes of theological systems which have been repressed.

I shall begin with Hitler's Third Reich. Adolph Hitler was raised as a Catholic, and, if he had become a priest, he would have been intellectually brilliant enough to ascend the ecclesiastical hierarchy, perhaps to the very top. Instead he encountered a situation in Germany in which the people collectively were suffering from the humiliation of defeat in World War I and the terms of the Versailles Treaty. During the 1930s, as is well known, Germany had become bankrupt and subject to an international embargo with respect to rearming and ever again menacing Europe. Hence, briefly put, the environment was favorable for the emergence of a messiah or savior figure, one who would transform its compliant status in the world to one of dominance while finding suitable scapegoats or sacrificial victims to atone for the malaise that had befallen the nation. Hitler promised to redeem Germany from its state of chaos and shame and to bring a new order to the world.

Hitler read the zeitgeist of the collective Germanic psyche impeccably and gave its youth both state-sanctioned identity and an outlet for aggression in militaristic forms and in devotion to him as an omnipotent father figure and quasi-numinous, though dark, messiah. The Nuremberg rallies with their torchlight parades, swastikas, the endless chanting of "Sieg Heil," and adrenalin-pumping oratory from the Führer himself were blatant religious rituals designed to resurrect Germanic myths and replace Christianity with the gods of pagan antiquity. Even before the outbreak of World War II in 1939, the myth of Aryan supremacy had become a justification for scapegoating and ethnically cleansing the Jews, the mentally ill, and other groups considered to contaminate the purity of the German race.

Jung thought of Hitler as an incarnation of the dark side of God and evidence of the reality of an almost metaphysical evil principle. Toward the end of *Memories, Dreams, Reflections,* Jung wrote:

Light is followed by shadow, the other side of the Creator. This development reached its peak in the twentieth century. The Christian world is now truly confronted by the principle of evil, by naked injustice, tyranny, lies, slavery, and coercion of conscience. This manifestation of naked evil has assumed apparently permanent form in the Russian nation; but its first violent eruption came in Germany. That outpouring of evil revealed to what extent Christianity has been undermined in the twentieth century. In the face of that, evil can no longer be minimized by the euphemism of the *privatio boni*. Evil has become a determinant reality. (1961, 328–329)

In this passage Jung is referring to the manifest evil in both Hitler's Third Reich and the former Soviet Union under Stalin. Paradoxically the holocaust was rationalized in part at least with the anti-Semitic myth that the Jews collectively had committed deicide by crucifying Christ, the symbol of the Light of God that had become human through the incarnation. The essential point is that Hitler's National Socialism was a theology, albeit one manifesting the savior archetype in a dark and sinister form, imposed on Europe by military intervention while enacting a fantasy of world domination. Hitler's God delusion was that imposing the Third Reich upon humanity was the expression of his own numinous and transcendent destiny, as though Hitler himself was an incarnation of God. Needless to say, perhaps, he despised the Bolsheviks, communism, and his equally deluded rival Joseph Stalin.

God and the Marxist Revolution

It might well be a supreme irony, though one which illustrates my point, that one of the most inspiring movies made about Christ was directed by a Marxist who depicted Jesus as a revolutionary pitted against the religious establishment of his time and the imperialist Roman occupiers as well. The film, *The Gospel According to St. Matthew*, was directed by Pier Paolo Pasolini, an atheist and Marxist whose depiction of Christ was nevertheless reverential. Pasolini, at a press conference, referred to himself as "an unbeliever with a nostalgia for belief" and announced that his film was "dedicated to the joyous, familiar memory of Pope John XXIII" who had invited a new dialogue with non-Catholic artists. The movie struck the right archetypal chords in the collective unconscious, portraying Christ as a hero, deliverer, and liberator of the oppressed people, especially the poor and socially marginalized who, in the Sermon on the Mount, would inherit the earth. Thus interpreted, the Christian myth and model of society had preceded that of Marxist philosophy by nineteen hundred years. Perhaps such ideational affinity helps to explain the Marxist sympathies of certain Jesuits in South America, including the rector of a university in El Salvador, Father Ignacio Ellacuria, who is rumored to have been murdered by U.S.-trained elite military units, as was Archbishop Oscar Romero, known as the "voice of the voiceless people" of this tragic country. Romero, though not himself a Marxist, used radio broadcasts and sermons to denounce the oppression, disappearance, and murder of political dissidents, including six Jesuits, by the ruling neofascist regime in El Salvador (Chomsky 2002, 165–167).

Theological minimalism did not diminish the power of the archetypal themes expressed in such lives. Marx, however, wanted to dispense with theology completely because he perceived religious orthodoxy as perpetuating social and economic injustice. Joseph Stalin took up Marx's project to an extreme degree, blowing up cathedrals, suppressing and murdering numerous clergy, and prohibiting religious teaching. Like Hitler, Stalin was a dictator, transforming Marxism into the ideology of a totalitarian state in which the persecution of intellectual dissidents would have appalled Marx, who saw himself as a liberator rather than promoting totalitarianism. Dissidents in both science and the arts, after show trials designed to induce fear in the people, were either executed, sent to gulags, or confined to mental asylums as social "schizophrenics," silenced with drugs such as reserpine.

Stalin had acquired his hero status during World War II, allying himself with Churchill and Roosevelt against the axis powers, especially Nazi Germany. He took credit for the victories of his generals, some of whom became victims of the dictator's paranoia and megalomania, along with an estimated six million people who were murdered as enemies of the state, sacrificial victims of a man who had once studied to become a priest but became inflated by identifying his ego consciousness with the numinous hero and savior archetypes. Stalin had many of his political adversaries, as well as dissident scientists and artists, put on trial for revisionism in relation to Marxist doctrine, and yet his own cult of personality to the extent of self-deification and perversion of Marxist principles was among the most egregious and oppressive of all "revolutionary" movements.

Instead of implementing the dictatorship of the proletariat and economic equality, Stalin and his comrades became the new and privileged aristocracy in place of the Tsarist regime, which had been liquidated during the revolution of 1917. The people suffered from poverty and recurring famines from which comrade Stalin was supposed to deliver them even as the religion of the state corrupted science and the humanities alike, as stories such as that of Nobel laureate and physicist Andrei Sakharov attest. Under Stalin, Soviet scientists are reputed to have pressured physicist Niels Bohr to revise his position on the Copenhagen interpretation of quantum physics by playing down the role of the mind of the observer, because of the implied embarrassment to the dogma of dialectical materialism that would be created by acknowledging the observer's consciousness (Laurikainen 1988, 58).

A further expression of the religion of the state was the embalming of Lenin, who remains in this immortalized bodily form in the Kremlin even after the restoration of religious and scientific freedom. Comrade Stalin's reign of terror is rumored to have ended when he was poisoned with a piece of his favorite chocolate cake. By becoming God, Stalin had betrayed the Marxist revolution while incarnating his own repressed and unconscious theism. A massive return of the repressed and resurrection of religious freedom would await the collapse of the Soviet Union and the return of the sweet smell of incense in the cathedrals, which had been preserved as museums to an outdated theology and presumably dead God.

The Cult of Chairman Mao

One further example should be sufficient to demonstrate that the dialectical materialism of Marxism does not dispense with God or numinous experience but simply changes the theology and outward appearances of religion in the form of the state and its unmistakably deified leaders. This example is the phenomenon of the cult of Chairman Mao. After defeating and ousting the Nationalists, the People's Liberation Army headed by Mao Tse-Tung began the project of eliminating China's imperial past and establishing a Marxist-Leninist state.

As had been the case with the new order in the Soviet Union, this entailed thoroughly embracing the ideology of dialectical materialism and the active suppression of all religion as a reactionary vestige of feudalism that had kept the people in poverty and servitude for centuries. Tibet was annexed, becoming a province of China, and the Dalai Lama forced into exile as a potentially subversive figure with respect to the propagation of communist dogma and social organization. Even in recent times pressure from the communist Chinese regime has resulted in refusal by countries such as South Africa to provide visas to the Dalai Lama, for instance, to visit his fellow Nobel Peace laureate emeritus Archbishop Desmond Tutu. Religion and theism, for the communist regime, were not simply delusional but a potential threat which had to be annihilated.

Compulsory withdrawal from the opiate of religion was essential to recovery from the malaise of past superstition and the uncritical acceptance of party propaganda so that the Long March toward a Marxist paradise could be completed. As the sun was setting on China's past, an opera titled *The East Is Red* celebrated the rise of Chairman Mao as the savior of his people and their new birth in a world in which the thoughts confined to a "little red book" became a barely disguised materialist, and terrifyingly militant, theology.

One of the symbols associated with Mao is the sunflower, linked with the God archetype and having much the same unconscious meaning as the rose window in a Gothic cathedral or the lotus flower of Buddhism. In Jungian depth psychology, sunflower, rose window, and lotus are all mandalas and symbols of inner wholeness, integration, and revivification of the Self.

In short, from the beginning, Chairman Mao was effectively deified by his people from whom blind obedience and mindless faith in communist doctrine were expected, ostensibly to fulfill the goals and quotas of the revolution. Dissenters and revisionists were dealt with harshly, with penalties ranging from summary execution or being beaten up by the Red Guards of the 1960s Cultural Revolution to exile in labor camps. The promised land, promoted by the ruling elite of comrades established and sustained in absolute power by the Red Army, became the new opiate of the people, which enabled them to endure endless famines as well as the mass murder of an estimated forty million of them for alleged crimes against the Orwellian state.

Until recent years, private ownership and enterprise were

condemned as corrupt capitalist practices while cultural influences from the West were subject to severe censorship to protect the people from contamination as they conformed to a work ethic that enabled them to achieve great leaps forward for China and, of course, for Chairman Mao. The depersonalization of human beings led to quotas being placed upon the number of children permitted per family, with compulsory abortion the price to be paid for miscalculations.

The cult of Chairman Mao was such that young people voyeuristically imitated him, for example, in the celebrated swim the old man took across the Yangtze River. Amulets, supposed to magically confer Mao's protection (even in death) were placed in automobiles much as in Western societies religious people have used crucifixes or icons of the Madonna. During the 1960s, young people in the West with Marxist sympathies, rebelling against religion, venerated the thoughts of Chairman Mao and his vision of a classless future, probably without realizing that this system of ideas amounted to a materialist theology.

Thus, communism in China became a religion of the state with a deified, charismatic leader, even as the Communist Party persecuted such overtly religious people as Tibetan Buddhists in the name of the liberation promised by the dialectical materialism of Karl Marx. In fact, freedom from organized religion came at the price of mindless surrender to the articles of faith offered by the state whose conduct of trials against political dissidents rivaled those in Stalinist Russia. Contemporary China can still be construed as living in the shadow of Mao, who remains an iconic figure in spite of concessions to capitalism and enterprises destined to contribute massively to global warming. Investment of the state with numinous qualities has resulted in the desacralization of more than a billion people (who can be shot for misdemeanors and religious practices) and the earth itself.

Consumerism and Packaged Spirituality

In the Western world, the banishment of spirit from matter and the desacralization of science as well as the observer have resulted in several bizarre phenomena. Such phenomena are manifestations both of metaphysical materialism and of what I have referred to as the religion of matter—the philosophy in which the material world and its resources acquire, via unconscious projection of denied and split-off psychic attributes, numinous qualities. By analogy to the great Gothic cathedrals that once encoded in stone the soaring spiritual aspirations of the medieval period, structures such as the twin towers of the World Trade Center became symbols cast in glass and steel of consumerism and of its capitalist materialist god.

Tragic as the casualties of 9/11 were, the destruction of the World Trade Center demonstrated globally just how vulnerable and, in Buddhist terms, impermanent the values symbolically represented by the towers actually are in a world in which all living beings are figuratively quantum entangled and interconnected, a world in which a geopolitical holism and global consciousness need to replace the anachronistic fragmentation of militant nationalism and economic self-interest. As I have suggested, the dangers of global warming to which the 2,500 scientists responsible for the Intergovernmental Panel on Climate Change report have alerted humankind represent one of a number of salient summonses to such a transformation in collective awareness. Denialists are morally in much the same untenable position as scientists paid by tobacco companies to minimize the significance of cigarette smoking for lung cancer and heart disease or the pharmaceutical companies whose insistence on patent rights delayed the availability of affordable generic brands of antiretroviral drugs to HIV-infected persons in the developing world.

The grotesque creed summed up in the maxim, "Greed is good," expressed by Pentecostal televangelists and prophets has totally inverted the message of the gospel that is supposedly the source of their religious worship. Under this creed the poor would no longer inherit the earth. Instead, the rich and powerful perceive the resources of the earth as their entitlement as the elect or chosen people favored by God. However, this grandiose belief in entitlement may simply be an extreme case of either confusing or identifying materialist consumerism with religion, while justifying twenty-first-century holy wars.

In reality, the televangelists and the religious right could be construed as unconscious materialists who are devoted to consumerism as their credo while masquerading as defenders of the Christian faith in their strident insistence upon biblical literalism and hostility to empirical science. In teaching the scriptures as history rather than potentially vivifying myth and moral allegory, they remain in collective denial of the underlying materialism that they actually share with skeptics and atheists. Using spatial metaphors such as heaven and hell to depict the afterlife in fundamentalist traditions itself tends to be materialistic rather than exploring the timelessness of the unconscious dimensions of the Self and God image or archetype as both "eternal and unconditioned" as Archbishop Rowan Williams (2007) has suggested. The depth psychological notion that the unconscious dimensions of the Self are not spatiotemporally bound may be both compatible with and fruitful for such theological positions.

I would argue passionately that it is materialism and its conceptual cousin consumerism that represent a menace to the earth rather than a scientifically illuminated theology or awakened spirituality. Precisely because these doctrines imply a desacralization of the earth as well as of life and hence a tendency to deny phenomena such as global warming and pandemics such as HIV/ AIDS, tuberculosis, and malaria as inconvenient truths for the governments and corporations and for the economic security of the developed world.

I have already explored how the implicit doctrine of metaphysical materialism in science, or scientism, indirectly supports these forms of religious psychopathology that are manifest in evangelically sanctioned consumerism. In scientism, the devotion is ostensibly to the material laws of nature, which have acquired numinous significance to the extent that mind and consciousness, until the quantum revolution in physics, was dismissed as being outside the domain of proper scientific enquiry. Investigations of the mental and of consciousness itself were condemned and exorcised as pseudoscience.

In the present context, it may be worth reminding ourselves that metaphysical materialism is a quasi-religious doctrine about nature rather than an account, for instance, in mathematical equations, of the laws of nature. As I explained in chapter 1, materialist doctrine defines what nature is permitted to be, not what can be discovered by science about nature. Thus, such dogma can preclude observation as well as being a set of canons about what is allowed into the domain of science. However, as Jung put it, that which had been cast out of the observer would find its way, via projection, into the material world itself. In his essay, "Psychology and Religion," Jung wrote: "If the historical process of world despiritualization continues as hitherto, then everything of a divine or daemonic nature outside us must return to the psyche, to the inside of the unknown man whence it originated. The materialistic error was probably unavoidable at first. Since the throne of God could not be discovered among the galactic systems, the inference was that God never existed" (1940, 85).

Another strange phenomenon, which could be construed as a symptomatic expression of materialism, is what I refer to as "packaged spirituality" for which consumers are willing to part with large amounts of money in ways that are uncannily reminiscent of the indulgences that once provided the wealthy with the illusion of salvation by the shilling. The abuse of indulgences became such a scandal that Martin Luther, who had been an Augustinian friar, regarded this and other corrupt practices as justification for the sixteenth-century Reformation.

Packaged spirituality caters to the often barely articulated, almost subliminal longing for self-transcendence and meaning that characterizes those in the Western world who have become disillusioned in religious orthodoxy yet remain, as Jung noted during the 1930s, "in search of a soul" (1933). The symbols and rituals of Christianity leave many experiencing neither authentic redemption nor rebirth. Jung and his colleagues such as Joseph Campbell have contributed much to salvaging such symbols and rituals from meaninglessness by exploring and recovering their archetypal roots in the collective unconscious. Hence, like mathematical truths, they retain their timelessness and eternal significance for the Self.

The nature of the unfulfilled and unconscious longing to which packaged spirituality is marketed is nothing less than the sublime experience of the *unio mystica* (mystical union) itself, described in the poetry and songs of the great mystics of both East and West. In the West, the writings of Hildegard of Bingen, Teresa of Ávila, and John of the Cross capture the rapturous and rejuvenating nature of the experience, as Jung and his followers, such as Michael Fordham (1985), attest. The unconscious thirst for inner transformation is exploited in advertising for products as diverse as vacations and shampoo.

Richard Dawkins's suggestion that the experiences of mystics are just by-products or disguised expressions of erotic love is as wide of the mark of understanding, I suggest, as would be the suggestion that Michelangelo's frescoes in the Sistine Chapel were due to his alleged homoeroticism. Naïve literalism clearly misses the point made, for instance, by Freud in formulating the concept of sublimation as an underpinning of culture as well as Jung's emphasis upon the transforming power and energy of numinous symbols. To Fordham, John of the Cross, as a spiritual director, was a medieval ancestor of today's Jungian analyst, acting as a catalyst of patients' inner transformation in the crucible of psychotherapy. Packaged spirituality, like the creative people in advertising agencies, offers the promise of transformation and dreams of a restored or new life downloaded in bytes by more or less charismatic individuals considered to be attractive on today's personality market.

An evening or seminar with such a personality, marketed as a guru or avatar and a source of almost instant enlightenment, is paid for with much the same mindlessness as indulgences for the remission of sin were paid for during the medieval period. Like most other products on the personal growth market, these imitation spiritual gems offer an instant and usually transient gratification, leaving the novice spiritually empty in the long run and still on an elusive quest for awakening, transformation, and wholeness.

Authentic mystical experience and the inner transformation facilitated by analytically oriented psychotherapies can neither be successfully marketed as instant remedies for the spiritual malaise and bankruptcy of the West nor commodified as objects or products purchasable at going rates. As I noted during the recent marketing of the Dalai Lama's visit to Australia, Buddhism is not some thing that can be consumed or digested as spiritual nourishment without years of devoted practice. Neither enlightenment nor inner transformation through encountering symbols of the Self and God archetype in the unconscious are possible without an experience of the shadow, of the dark night of the soul in which the darkness is at its most visible and tangible just prior to the experience of the light.

This is as clearly the case with the disciplined rigor and ritual of psychoanalytic psychotherapy oriented toward the restoration and transformation of the Self as it is for the lifelong commitment of spiritual practice. Focused short-term solutions to problems in living, and some forms of "mindfulness" training can amount to little more than thought magic, at least in unprofessional hands. As a recent movie script, "What the Bleep Do We Know!?" put it, "if your thoughts can create symmetrical patterns in water, imagine what they can do to you." No experimental data published in peer-reviewed journals were adduced to support this proposition.

In conclusion, packaged spirituality can be little more than an intrusive extension of materialist consumerism into the domain of the sacred. By offering an illusion of some form of instant enlightenment or inner transformation, such packaged products not only disguise their exploitative intent, they are also fraudulent insofar as they fail to deliver what they promise. Packaged spirituality creates an illusion of embarking upon the journey to the center of one's being and an awakening to personal meaning, transcendence, and connection with the numinous. It has nothing to do with the reality of a living experience of God or with the notion that, perhaps beyond the brief span of this life, the arrow of time neither destroys mind nor ends the continuity of the Self. According to Schrödinger, who asked whether time destroyed the mind that constructed it, the arrow of time leaves mind indestructible. Death might be construed as a profound turning point or transformative experience. It is to this intriguing and perhaps shocking possibility that I now turn. I argue that it is nothing more than a materialist and reductionist prejudice that concludes that mind necessarily ends with the disintegration of the brain on the assumption that mind is to be simply identified with brain processes.

The Ending Which Is Also a Beginning

The eternal truths of mathematics and scientific laws expressed in equations of awesome beauty exist before they are discovered, as Schrödinger (1992) and Penrose (2004) have noted. Compared to John Polkinghorne (2006), I would place what he refers to as the "atemporality of God" into the category of experiences of illumination into eternal truths that are accessible to human beings in the here and now of this life, while also being integral to the experience of self-continuity after death. Polkinghorne's idea that the informational patterns, which he regards as defining the human soul, somehow dissolve at death but are held "in Divine memory (by God) with the intention of reconstitution" in a physical body through "the divine eschatological act of Resurrection" at the end of time seems to me to come perilously close to materialism while denying spiritual survival (2006, 49). Is one to construe the "soul's pattern" held in "Divine memory," which Polkinghorne describes, as conscious or simply as a form of active information without the attributes of either consciousness or identity? Is this divine memory or Polkinghorne's God to be found anywhere in space and time?

However, it is the more profound implication of Schrödinger's idea that the arrow of time leaves mind indestructible which I wish to explore more fully here. From the perspective of the orthodox religion of materialism, such a notion would be considered either grossly heretical or, to someone like Richard Dawkins, scientific apostasy, even though the nature of mind and its irreducibility to matter have been explored by such luminaries as Schrödinger, Penrose, Bohm, and Pauli. The ending of radical materialism, which marked the beginning of a restored scientific focus upon the mind of the observer, dates from the early twentieth century rise of psychoanalysis and the quantum revolution in physics. The exploration of the unconscious by Freud and Jung and the meaningfully coincidental discovery of the role of the personal equation or consciousness of the human observer in quantum physics would mean questioning strict neo-Darwinism in biology while permitting solution of Wallace's problem with the inconvenient anomaly of mind in the theory of evolution. It may not be widely known that Schrödinger had a great deal to say about subjects ostensibly outside the scope of physics, such as the origins of life, mind, consciousness, science, and religion.

As for God, Schrödinger noted, somewhat scathingly, that a materialistic science that had banished anything personal from its universe as an a priori condition could not therefore expect to discover such an entity within the space and time coordinates of the cosmos. Nor could the genius of Schrödinger himself under such circumstances, so he turned to the writings of Eastern mystics for inspiration about both God and mind.

Similarly, the mind of the observer, responsible for the magnificent construction of the edifice of science itself had, by some form of bizarre or schizoid logic, to be disregarded as a subject of legitimate empirical investigation and denied the predicate of existence. Such delusions could only be maintained in the classical, mechanistic physics of Newton. They could no longer be ignored when the mind and consciousness of the observer intruded themselves into the experiments of quantum theory in the form of undeniable effects. A complete physics must provide an account of the observer, as Pauli, Penrose, and many others have noted in writing about the mental and consciousness.

These considerations seem to have been so exasperating to Richard Dawkins that he emphasized that the famous paradox of Schrödinger's cat had been invented merely as a satirical comment on the Copenhagen interpretation of quantum theory, with its notion of the interaction between the observer and the observed. The Schrödinger's cat story is a simplified account or analogy of the concept of superposition states of particles as well as the role of the observer in reflecting upon such matters as possibly simultaneous "dead" and "alive" states. The term *superposition* in quantum physics denotes the existence of multiple alternative states, for instance, of particles, or in biology of mutated and nonmutant forms of a microorganism rather than a macroscopic object like a cat.

In the much-quoted Schrödinger's cat paradox, the fate of the animal in a closed box depends on a quantum mechanical event that determines whether or not a cyanide capsule is opened, with a 50 percent probability of this event occurring. Without opening the box, the cat is considered to be in a superposition of dead and alive states. A more technical account of this set up is beyond the scope of this book and available in popular accounts of quantum physics. Roger Penrose, in *The Emperor's New Mind,* presented a popular account of different points of view among physicists concerning the paradox of Schrödinger's cat and of the role of the observer (1999, 375–388). Penrose also said, "A fundamental physical theory that lays claim to any kind of completeness must also have the potential to accommodate conscious mentality" (2004, 1033). This view is consistent with Pauli's position concerning the personal equation or mind of the observer in quantum physics outlined by Laurikainen (1988, 58–62) and discussed in chapters 2 and 3.

The arrow of time, as Schrödinger and others since have pointed out, is a construct of the mind. As such a construct, the arrow of time leaves the mind of its creator as indestructible as the immutable and eternal truths of the mathematics that it also discovers often with a rapture that skeptics, with their high index of suspicion for anything spiritual, might well regard as an epiphenomenal spin-off or by-product of something else, such as erotic desire. One embarrassing difficulty for skeptics, however, is that mind cannot be confined to a priori categories or coordinates of space and time, which are themselves mental constructions. Only the conscious, intentional, and purely rational aspects of mental activity can be construed in this limited way.

The nonalgorithmic and noncomputable aspects of intelligence and creativity cannot be so understood, and yet it is these that are responsible for epiphanies in mathematics and science referred to as Archimedean experiences and which seem difficult to explain only in terms of their survival value in Darwinian evolution. I have already argued at some length that the unconscious dimensions of mind and of the Self are not bound by space and time.

Furthermore, if the alleged destructibility of the mind with the disintegration of the matter of the brain is contingent upon the strict confinement of the mental to space and time, then the rationalist notion of the extinction of the Self at death is a delusion. So also is the often unquestioned identification of mind with brain processes and events according to the so-called identity hypothesis otherwise known as reductionist or eliminative materialist "neuroism." However, this means the beginning of the end for materialism and for the delusions about God.

It is time now to dispel these delusions and to return to the timeless reality known as the unconscious and pre-spacetime alluded to earlier in discussing the complementarity of physics and depth psychology and contributions from neuroscience. I have argued in chapters 3 and 4 that an evolving theology can be enriched greatly by contributions from other disciplines, especially perhaps, analytical and depth psychology. These considerations may facilitate the quest for a theology of the third millennium in which science and religion are no longer split or divorced but rather integrated and perceived as perspectives standing in a relationship of complementarity to one another.

CHAPTER 6

A Third-Millennium Theology

Paradoxically, evangelical and fundamentalist theology has remained bound by the categories of space and time as well as a cosmology from the pre-Copernican period of history. It remains a dogmatic and doctrinal theology that is suspicious of mysticism and science alike. This almost paranoid theological posture is an ever-present obstacle to overcoming the schism between science and religion that has existed since the seventeenth century. Wolfgang Pauli wrote of the need for a reintegration of repressed "spirit" into science, in particular that of Jungian depth psychology, so that lost wholeness could be restored according to the archetype of the *coniunctio oppositorum* or union of opposites. The schism is one that provides skeptics and agnostics such as Richard Dawkins with copious ammunition for the argument that God is a delusion rooted in such absurdities as the doctrine of intelligent design and alleged refutations of the theory of evolution.

At its worst, evangelical and fundamentalist theology literalizes spatial metaphors about the "location" of God in the heavens, teaching the scriptures as history and postponing any experience of the timeless or eternal to a future beyond death. Erwin Schrödinger's description of pictorial representations of heaven, hell, and purgatory in medieval art as "materialistic" effectively captures the result of such concretism and literalism (1992, 140). It is the species of theology from which science had to separate and liberate itself because they precluded the revelation of truth through the free pursuit of empirical research. The God of such archaic theologies had to die in order to be resurrected with the primordial energy and timeless quality of the unconscious archetype, stripped of anthropomorphic garments and animistic projection, while expressing rich symbolic meaning. What is required is nothing less than a theology for the third millennium.

Such a theology will not, I believe, fill in ever-decreasing lacunae in the scientific explanation of the universe and the role of the human observer in the cosmos. Nor will it be a theology that simply

126

accommodates science uncomfortably because empirical realities such as evolution cannot be denied. The new theology will be illuminated by science while emerging from scientific understanding as if from a womb. It will be a case of science itself giving birth to concepts of the numinous that will stand, as I have suggested, in a relationship of complementarity to religion, in fulfilment of Albert Einstein's prediction that science would one day return humanity to God.

The shape of such a third-millennium theology will emerge from a more profound consideration of the role of mind and consciousness in evolution—from the quantum level through to humanity itself and even beyond the collective unconscious—and from an enhanced understanding of time.

The experience of the so-called arrow of time—in the face of which mind, according to Schrödinger, is indestructible—is so compelling in post-Newtonian Western society that the vast ocean of timelessness from which both mind and matter emerge is easily obscured or eclipsed from awareness. This may be why it is difficult for humankind in the West to grasp the experience of the great mystics, even those to whom physicists like Schrödinger and David Bohm have turned for insight into those profound dimensions of mind that transcend the spatiotemporal confines of rational classical, scientific systems of thought. And yet quantum physics and depth psychology alike confront scientists with aspects of reality that are both irrational and timeless, only becoming manifest in time as particles or archetypal dream symbols while revealing their origins in Bohm's implicate order or in C. G. Jung's unconscious archetypes as cosmic ordering and regulating principles.

If mind and matter are disentangled and complementary aspects of an original primordial, unitary, and timeless reality (the *unus mundus*), then the religion of reductionist materialism is false. That leaves theology and science with the challenge of exploring the implications of mind, neither destructible nor spatiotemporally bound, yet infinite in extent. Roger Penrose (1999, 2004), as noted in chapters 2 and 3, has described mathematical solutions that are rapturously and radiantly beautiful in virtually mystical language and, like those of Schrödinger, exist eternally prior to their discovery by human beings.

Such radiant wisdom might just as well be described as numinous in nature and origin, and yet it is of its nature an epiphany to the human consciousness that reflects upon it, frequently as an apparent law of the universe revealing itself to the human mirror which the cosmos has evolved. Thus perhaps we can begin to see that God becomes incarnate in humanity, not from some remote and external source, but from within evolving matter itself, as its interior aspect becoming conscious in and through that selfsame humankind. This, however, is already an incipient theology, though one in which the *unio mystica* is inseparable from a God that has been becoming human for all eternity. Such a God whose incarnation continues through humanity is transpersonal, not impersonal, and, as an archetype, is not bound by space and time, as I have argued in chapter 4.

Theology, though not fully inseminated by the notions of time emerging from physics and depth psychology, seems nevertheless to have juxtaposed the finite and temporal with the eternal and infinite in its attempts to find meaning in the human condition and its role in the cosmos. In contemplating the intersection of the temporal and eternal, traditional theology in the West has tended to focus on such apparently supernatural interventions as the incarnation of Christ in history while postponing the ultimate questions of self-continuity and eternal life to a speculative form of being after death. The highly imaginative constructions about the nature of this future eternal state of being could be construed as themselves remarkable creative expressions of the human mind and even as certain archetypes of the collective unconscious, if subject to much the same sort of analytic interpretation as the symbolic content of the dreams of patients undergoing psychotherapy.

Archetypal images and themes in the dreams and collective mythologies of humankind do provide intimations of eternity because of their origin in a timeless and primordial order. I would argue that the more sophisticated forms of theology in both West and East could be viewed as examples of such mythology, with a deeper wisdom for humankind, analogous to the significance of dreams for patients in psychoanalysis provided they are understood symbolically rather than being concretized or taught as literal or historical truths.

The Genesis story has been taught in fundamentalist theologies as historical reality rather than myth, and Jung himself noted that the historic Christ has been eclipsed both by the collective projection of archetypal material onto him and by the efforts of the theological mythmakers for two millennia. The crucified Christ perceived as a reconciling symbol uniting the opposites of good and evil, light and darkness, within the collective human psyche might well make more psychological and theological sense than the primitive notion of a human sacrifice, the purpose of which is to atone for the sins of humankind against a wrathful patriarchal deity.

The incarnation of God in humanity may acquire a more sublime and contemporary meaning if it is to be understood not as a dogmatic assertion about a singular historic event but rather, as I have suggested in chapters 3 and 4, as a sublime symbolic expression of the participation of humanity in an evolutionary process of completing God. This insight, I believe, captures the numinous dimension of humanity instead of perpetuating a myth in which God remains remote, separate, and supernatural rather than representing the transcendence of which humankind is naturally capable, through creating in science and mathematics and in artistic masterpieces.

In this respect, it may be worth noting that in Michelangelo's fresco the primordial man represented in Adam is of similar stature to the God by whom he was created in the myth depicted in the Christian scriptures. Michelangelo's Adam seems to be represented magnificently, as a fully potent and equal partner with God in cocreation, not as infantile, vulnerable, and dependent, a posture that tends to be perpetuated by traditional, dogmatic theology.

Another example of the fruitful application of analytical, depth-psychological interpretation to mythology and theological dogma was provided by Jung in his memoirs. As a young man, Jung was so miffed by his father's refusal to respond adequately to his questions about the Trinity that Jung's unconscious produced a dream in which the father-God defecated upon his own cathedral in Basel: the cathedral was blown apart by a gigantic turd.

Many years later, in 1952, a more enlightened Jung expressed delight in an event which, if interpreted literally, was simply a proclamation of religious and dogmatic absurdity. I am referring to the formal pronouncement by Pope Pius XII of the bodily assumption of the Virgin Mary as a dogma binding upon Catholics. Jung's delight was in the symbolic significance of the uniting of the archetypal and eternal feminine and of the earth with the masculine Trinity. To Jung, this event was a ritualized and collective vindication of his archetype of the *coniunctio oppositorum* and wholeness of the Self, irrespective of any theological or metaphysical significance. Jung's aim was to restore meaning to the symbols, not to dismiss theology, although phenomenologically, he did not believe that it was possible to distinguish symbols of the deeper Self from the unconscious God image. In "Answer to Job," Jung wrote: "In recognition of this truth and evidently inspired by the workings of the Holy Ghost, the Pope has recently announced the dogma of the *Assumptio Mariae*, very much to the astonishment of all rationalists" (1952a, 458). In the chapter in *Aion* titled "The Sign of the Fishes," Jung referred to "the solemn proclamation of the *Assumptio Mariae* as an example of the way symbols develop through the ages" (1951, 87), including the *imago Dei* or God archetype, about which he wrote: "Strictly speaking the God image does not coincide with the unconscious as such but with a special content of it, namely the archetype of the Self. It is this archetype from which we can no longer distinguish the God image empirically" (1951, 469). In his various formulations, Jung made it clear that his empirical statements were not intended to circumvent such Christian mysteries as that of the incarnation of God in Christ celebrated in the liturgy of the mass.

Dawkins, on the other hand, approaches such phenomena not for what they may be expressing symbolically about the human condition but literally, paradoxically falling into the same errors as the religious fundamentalists of whose concreteness and stupidity he is thoroughly convinced. Incidentally, in his scathingly critical remarks about such phenomena as falling in love "with a wafer" in reference to the Christian Eucharist (2006, 186), one could be forgiven for asking who commits the greater error of concretism in relation to grasping symbols. Dawkins? Or those for whom the transformational drama of the Eucharistic rite represents communion with and active participation in a mystery of transcendent and numinous significance beyond themselves? (See chapter 5 for a discussion of the archetypal, symbolic aspects of the mass as a transformation ritual and passion play.)

Similarly, an enormous difference in attitude exists between perceiving the great Gothic cathedrals of Notre Dame and Chartres with their rose windows as merely aesthetically pleasing, geometrical works in stone and colored glass rather than as cosmic, archetypal mandala symbols of wholeness, harmony, and balance within the human psyche, associated with numinous feelings of awe and rapture awakened by a sense of connection with the divine.

I now turn to a reassessment of time from the perspective of science, especially depth psychology and physics, in order to consider ways in which a reevaluation of Chronos might illuminate a third-millennium theology, in which the arrow of time does not necessarily mortally wound the mind (or Self) of its creator, scandalous as such a notion might be for religious materialists.

Mind from the Perspectives of Time and Eternity

In chapters 3 and 4, we considered the concept of time from such perspectives as those of depth psychology, quantum physics, and neuroscience without exploring the possible implications for a third-millennium theology. This deficit must now be remedied as traditional theology has yet to integrate these changes in the experience and conceptualization of time which have been the inevitable though unintended consequences of post-classical physics and the scientific understanding of the unconscious, particularly if the latter is thought to be coextensive with the universe itself. Even Darwin's theory of evolution shattered the rigid and constrained temporal framework that had characterized Western theology, particularly, for almost two millennia. Evangelical and fundamentalist theologies still cling to creationist beliefs about time that are not only known to be empirically false, but also fixed in prescientific myths and systems of thought.

Whereas skeptics like Dawkins and the metaphysical materialists generally regard the indestructibility or continuity of mind and of the Self as a delusion, I have argued the reverse case, namely, that the idea of their inevitable extinction is itself an illusion created by a misunderstanding of the arrow of time and a failure to grasp the implications of the timelessness of the unconscious psyche. The reality is that at its most profound levels mind is neither spatiotemporally bound nor reducible to matter. Yet logically, the destructibility of mind (and of the Self) is contingent upon both of these conditions being met.

Otherwise, the only honest choice is a twenty-first-century "theological" one, specifically, that mind must be considered as *sub specie aeternitatis,* that is to say, from the perspective of the eternal or timeless. I have already established, in discussing the work of Bohm and his colleague Basil Hiley in chapter 3, that even at the quantum level, mind exists as active information, though devoid of consciousness and furthermore that in his "undivided universe" Bohm postulated the existence of a Mind extending infinitely beyond that of the human collective (2002, 386).

Active information forms the bridge between the mental and the physical, neither of which can be reduced to the other. This is the relationship of complementarity between mind and matter described by Jung and Pauli, for whom the bridge consists of the archetypes as cosmic ordering and regulating principles. Bohm's concept of the implicate order and his idea of the quantum hologram imply influences independent of space and time, as does the idea of the archetypes of the collective unconscious, which are timeless in nature.

A primordial foundation or origin of both mind and matter that is characterized by timelessness implies that the Newtonian concept of absolute time needs to be replaced, even without the relativity revolution introduced by Einstein. Such concepts are also necessarily numinous and can potentially transform theology.

The idea that mind somehow ceases to exist with the disintegration of the brain is an illusion created by uncritical acceptance of classical, Newtonian concepts, including that of a clockwork mechanistic universe that is running down according to an unchallenged entropy. However, the negentropy upon which, in Schrödinger's terms, "life feeds," eventually creating the "contraption" of the human brain as the organ of reflective consciousness, is not some almost accidental and transient artifact in the universe. The application of Occam's razor entails the rejection of such a wasteful interpretation of the evolution of both the cosmos and life itself, which might well have required some form of quantum computing in tandem with adaptive or directed mutation to reach its current and observable level of complexity and consciousness of itself.

The distinction between those aspects of mind that are eternal or timeless and those bound by space and time is vital, I believe, for the development of a new theology illuminated by science. I shall begin my further elaboration of this theme by referring to an illustration of the principle provided by Karl Pribram (see also chapter 3). Pribram writes: "Particular stages of brain processes that organize vision operate in the unconscious spectral domain while our conscious experience is in spacetime" (2004, 19). He uses the analogy of fMRI (functional magnetic resonance imaging of the brain), "where the apparatus operates in the (timeless) quantum holographic domain while the resulting pictures emerge in spacetime" (ibid., 16). The pictures freeze

The only Freudian

the timeless holoflux within the coordinates of space and time in the form of still pictures of a dynamic process, much as images or ideas entering consciousness from the unconscious become frozen in space and time as symbolic representations for contemplation by the conscious mind and interpretation in psychoanalysis. Again, the reductionist illusion is that finite mental material frozen in spacetime either exhausts infinite Mind or implies its destruction. Pribram's philosophical position is, in his own words, "hostile to an eliminative, reductionist, materialist stance" (ibid., 8). Furthermore, Pribram argues that both mind and matter have a common ontological root, specifically, the "more fundamental order of a prespacetime potential that underlies and transcends spacetime" (ibid., 14).

This also is the stuff of which a scientifically informed theology can be made. Even more scandalous perhaps, for metaphysical materialists, Pribram defined the cultural world as "spiritual" in the sense that reflectively conscious human beings are attracted to patterns or "informational structures" beyond immediate daily concerns, which implies both a search for understanding and self-transcendence.

The informational structures to which Pribram refers can be as diverse as those of science and religion, in both of which, coincidentally perhaps, paradoxes in the understanding of time are confronted. Pribram finds much in common with philosopher Karl Popper (1983) for whom interaction among his "three worlds" of brain, culture, and mind achieve consciousness and ensure its future evolution as culture in the form of science, art, and even religion.

Comprehension of the ultimate destination or state of mind at the end of life, however, is contingent upon a more profound understanding of the arrow of time in juxtaposition with the various concepts of timelessness. This issue of whether time destroys the mind of its creator and the related question of self-continuity have been almost hopelessly entangled in the apparently unbreakable net of the so-called spatiotemporal hold, the tenacity of which is not changed by the paradoxes of relativity theory, in which the speed of light remains constant. Thus, the arrow of time associated with irreversible entropy and the "running down" of the universe has seemed to strangle any hope of continuity of mind or Self beyond death. In "A Psychological Approach to the Dogma of the Trinity," Jung wrote that the self in its totality could be represented by a mandala, an archetypal symbol of wholeness and integration. "The self is defined psychologically as the psychic totality of the individual. Anything that a man postulates as being a greater totality than himself can become a symbol of the self.... The goal of psychological as of biological development is self-realization or individuation. But since man knows himself only as an ego and the self as a totality is indescribable and indistinguishable from a God-image, self-realization—to put it in religious or metaphysical terms—amounts to God's incarnation" (Jung 1948, 156–157).

Later, Jungian analyst Michael Fordham, in a chapter titled "The Self in Jung's Works," wrote, concerning the archetype of the Self: "Certain of these images would be experienced as numinous and greater and more powerful than the ego. The forms may appear to symbolize a powerful integrative influence. As the development proceeds a centralizing process may be discerned which draws together the numinous images in the mandala form. That may be a summary of where integration has led the subject, and ultimately it can include the cosmos"(1985, 26). Fordham indicates that Jung's concept of "the ultimate" implied the existence of unconscious dimensions of the Self that transcend space and time (ibid., 33).

These notions, so important to theology, are profoundly relevant to the issues of self-continuity and immortality as well as the conceptualization of the numinous that is the central concern of theologians. Dawkins's final solution to answering such big picture or ultimate philosophical questions is quite simple: ridicule rather than reasoned debate. To Dawkins and other skeptics, such questions are not just imponderable, they are also empirically unknowable and as seemingly irrational as dream content, mythology, and the archetypal visions depicted in religious works of art, both Western and Eastern. The scientific understanding of time may become one of the utmost salience for the project of evolving a third-millennium theology. Equally salient may be Pribram's notion that science consists of multiple informational patterns, which transcend immediate temporal concerns while expressing a myth or archetype of supreme spiritual significance for humankind, that of the quest for *logos* or understanding of the Word. Was it not such divine knowledge that was forbidden in the Genesis myth?

Why is it, indeed, that mathematics and physics are found to belong to the realm of the timeless or eternal and human sources of wisdom in these disciplines have been given the symbolic status of prophets, seers, or heavenly messengers? If the mythic Prometheus stole fire from the gods, scientists and mathematicians experience epiphanies of timeless truths and empirical laws from an apparently eternal, Platonic realm described by physicists as eminent as Schrödinger, Pauli, Bohm, and Penrose.

Does Time Destroy Its Own Creator?

Schrödinger himself, after discussing the implications of the statistical theory of time, proposed that "what we in our minds construct, cannot have the power of annihilating mind" and that in his view, physical theory "strongly suggests the indestructibility of mind by time" (1992, 152). He was referring, among other things, to the categories of space and time that are mental constructs, as, for instance, are the quantum and relativity theories. The almost irresistible illusion that time does destroy its own creator is largely a result of the human experience, especially in rational, "enlightened" Western societies, of an apparently irreversible flow of time characteristic of the classical, mechanistic physics of Newton. By contrast, as outlined in chapter 4, the unconscious is not bound by space and time. Rather, it is characterized by timelessness, as are the archetypes of the collective unconscious described by Jung and his followers.

Rational consciousness is spatiotemporally bound, experiencing intimations of timelessness only in dreams, meditative states, great music, and moments of scientific, mathematical, and artistic inspiration. The linear flow of events from womb to tomb seems to be inescapable and inexorable, as though the end were present even at the beginning of life, which is, as Shakespeare put it, in the words of Prospero, "We are such stuff as dreams are made on and our little life is rounded with a sleep" (*The Tempest*, act 4, scene 1). Much as he or she may wish to be rescued from this predicament, the ordinary person secretly knows its lawfulness. After all, it is common sense that the sun rises in the morning and that therefore celestial bodies revolve around the Earth. It is a similar rational, "commonsense" belief that no experience exists beyond bodily death and the disintegration of the brain.

Such common sense, however, has not been illuminated by the insights of depth psychology, quantum physics, or even neuroscience with their notions of timelessness. The rejection of the reductionist materialism that I have described as such a menace to humanity and the acceptance of some notion of the complementarity or dual aspect monist nature of the mind and matter relationship render naïve realist concepts of the extinction of the human creator by its own construct of time difficult to sustain or at least questionable. So also does the acknowledgment of the so-called arrow of time as simply a ripple or wave that occurs on an otherwise timeless, boundless, and infinite ocean, with respect to mind in its unconscious aspects. I shall illustrate this point with an example.

Alzheimer's disease might, at first glance, seem to be a degenerative condition in which the continuity of the self is extinguished. However, adopting a view of the mind/matter problem that is one of complementarity rather than reductionist and materialist, I would argue that in a real sense self-continuity in such severely brain-damaged patients can be preserved in a way that is detectable, at least in some cases, in long-term memory, whereby the distant and remote past becomes reality in the present historic time, awareness of which has been lost. Thus the spatiotemporal hold is broken and in spite of appearances to the contrary, neither the degenerative process nor the arrow of time has destroyed the self of which time is a construct. To clinical observation, it is simply that the narrative "I" provides an account of those distant memories that now comprise its reality, as if time itself had been reversed for the patient. To the person's mind, a much loved symphony from the past may evoke the rapture of its first hearing during childhood and in recognition of the glorious cascade of sound, something eternal dissolves all sense of tensed (past, present, and future) time.

In other words, the more profound reality of mind is that it is timeless and eternal except for the personal experience of a life span and the historic reality represented in the emergence of humanity in the evolution of life on earth.

The same human species as noted in chapter 3 in discussing the work of Bohm (2002, 389), is the mirror which the universe has evolved to reflect upon itself, a reality, noted also by Schrödinger who asserted, "what we in our minds construct cannot, so I feel, have dictatorial power over our mind, neither the power of bringing it to the fore nor the power of annihilating it" (1992, 152). It is not that matter and time are purely illusory or solely the results of a psychological process of creating concepts and theories, on a quest for understanding self, species origins, and transpersonal meaning, which is spiritual in itself. The illusion is that matter and linear time somehow completely exhaust the reality of the universe and therefore eliminate their creator with death and bodily disintegration, instead of being perceived in their true nature as relative and as themselves explications of the mental. Without psyche, there would be no theory, including that of metaphysical materialism, nor would a being exist to discover the timeless mathematical truths to which physicists like Schrödinger have referred. Jung had come to a similar awakening, I believe, when he stated in his autobiographical *Memories, Dreams, Reflections* that "the most decisive question for a man is whether he is related to something infinite or not" (1961, 357). Concerning his own rapturous near death experience in 1942 Jung wrote, "A good many of my principal works were written only then…. It was only after the illness that I understood how important it is to affirm one's destiny" (ibid., 328).

If there is a Mind extending indefinitely beyond even that of the collective consciousness of humanity in which human beings participate and if this reality transcends space and time, then destruction of its creator by time is a logical contradiction, besides being existentially improbable. A phrase that specifically captures this is the notion of the timelessness/permanence pole of the experiencing subject proposed by the philosopher Shalom (1989) in his book on personal identity. A dimension of the human subject or identity that is both permanent and timeless necessarily implies a form of immortality, as Shalom suggests in his treatment of the question of self-continuity beyond death. Specifically, he wrote, "What we call self-consciousness is the explicit manifesting to itself of the timelessness-permanence pole of human subjectivity" (1989, 482). Shalom noted that "an existence which evolves a subject capable of questioning its own evolution and capable of understanding much of the universe itself…. Is not possible without a God" (ibid., 485).

The implicate order of Bohm and the archetypal cosmic ordering and regulating principles explored by Pauli and Jung speak to humanity of a reality that transcends spacetime, and by partaking in it human beings experience something of the eternal, even in this life, to which, as Jung put it, a question is brought, its answer sought in the realm of the temporal. The answer to this question is transpersonal and something that connects the individual to the infinite.

In the end, Jung came to perceive that the collective unconscious was but an internal reflection or mirror of the external cosmos, potentially infinite in its extent, while Schrödinger, disillusioned by Western religion and theology, turned to the mystical traditions of the East for spiritual enlightenment and a more profound understanding of mind. This experience might well have provided him with the focused clarity with which he came to perceive space and time as constructs and the mind as indestructible by what he humorously referred as the "tyranny of Chronos" (Schrödinger 1992, 152).

In any case and as an unintended consequence, Schrödinger may have contributed to a theology and understanding of the numinous remarkably fit for the third millennium. The theology would be incarnational, in something like the sense proposed by Teilhard de Chardin but stripped of the notion of a deity somehow intervening in history to become human in order to redeem a disordered creation. I now turn to outlining this theology with the additional comment that such a theology would be truly universal (rather than tribal) in its embrace of the archetypal, spiritual treasure contained in humankind's great religious traditions, both Western and Eastern.

Humankind Completing God

The discovery of a cultural and extrabiological transmission of information was, according to biologists such as Julian Huxley and Theodosius Dobzhansky, an evolutionary discovery of unparalleled significance for humankind. In his introduction to Teilhard de Chardin's *The Phenomenon of Man*, Huxley wrote, "With his conception of mankind as an unfinished product of past evolution and an agency of distinctive evolution to come... he wanted to deal with the entire human phenomenon as a transcendence of biological by psychosocial evolution" (in Teilhard de Chardin 1959, 24). Huxley wrote of Teilhard: "Through his combination of wide scientific knowledge with deep religious feeling and a rigorous set of values, he has forced theologians to view their ideas in the new perspective of evolution and scientists to see the spiritual implications of their knowledge" (ibid., 26). Dobzhansky, at the conclusion of *Evolution, Genetics, and Man*, wrote of humanity that "one species made an evolutionary discovery of unparalleled significance; the extrabiological transmission of acquired and learned experience. This species became human and opened up a new cultural or human evolution. About two thousand years ago this species had advanced far enough to receive the Sermon on the Mount.... Julian Huxley thinks that man finds himself in the unexpected position of business manager for the cosmic process of evolution" (1963, 378). However, the spiritual quest for understanding and meaning, resulting in a cascade of insights into the origins and future direction of the species, sets humanity apart from all other living species, including the primates, as does the extraordinary awakening into the reality that humankind is indeed the universe evolved enough to reflect upon itself. David Bohm, commenting upon the ontological interpretation of quantum physics, wrote: "There is no need to regard the observer as basically separate from what he sees nor to reduce him to an epiphenomenon of the objective process. More broadly one could say that through the human being the universe is making a mirror to observe itself" (2002, 389). Humankind does not simply passively contemplate, but actively decodes the laws of physics, classical and quantum, as well as those which govern the emergence of life and eventually the complexity of Mind itself. It is the notion of human beings as actors rather than mere spectators that I wish to develop further as a theme directly relevant to a third-millennium theology.

Eminent physicists and biologists, as well as depth psychologists like Jung and Fordham, have all commented on the role of human beings as actors, participants, and creators in the evolutionary process that resulted in the species, following a number of prehominid ancestors. According to the traditional neo-Darwinian paradigm, the doctrine of the natural selection of chance variations still prevails in spite of incommensurable evidence. However, with the acknowledgment of such phenomena as global warming and of an undeniable anthropogenic contribution, the notion of humanity being collectively responsible for the future of the earth may be a catalyst for transformation in consciousness conducive to a specieswide embrace of Teilhard de Chardin's noosphere.

Furthermore, humankind confronts the transcendence immanent and implicit in the cosmic history of the universe and apparently manifest in an infinite and eternal Mind as well. And yet, paradoxically, in the experience of an apparently eternal now, the majestic, awesome, and glorious task in which humanity is participating is nothing less than that of completing the incarnation of God in historic time. Teilhard de Chardin was silenced for proposing a similar vision of the future of humanity, actively and industriously creating a noosphere or envelope of consciousness and meaning around the closed curvature of the earth. He was silenced, perhaps, because his evolutionary theology brought God down from the figurative heavens and into such a close intimacy and identification with humanity that God's omnipotent and omniscient qualities and transcendence of the creation, depicted in Genesis and enshrined in dogma, would be called into question.

Teilhard, I suspect, saw with remarkable clarity what the theologians of his time had missed, even though it hovered above them in the Sistine Chapel: the mature and empowered stature of the primordial Adam in relation to the generative father-God. However, removed from the traditional, interventionist stance in theology, the incarnation of God in cosmic evolution implies that God becomes fully conscious through and is completed by humankind in a *unio mystica* of perhaps unexpected significance. As Teilhard put it, "Erit in omnibus in omnia Deus," which means that God may become all in and through all. Alternatively, humankind could evolve in such a way as to fulfill the divine potential of completing the incarnation of God.

The silencing of Teilhard may have been rooted in part on an unconscious fear that the notion of God becoming human might also lead to a possible inflation through the assertion of its corollary, namely, that somehow humankind could become divine and endowed with the Logos. This idea is anticipated in such scriptural sayings as the opening chapter in the Gospel of John: "And the Light shineth in the darkness and the darkness comprehended it not.... That Light was the true Light which lighteth every man that cometh into the world.... But as many as received Him, to them He gave the power to become the sons of God" (1:1–12 KJV). This statement is very close to the theological position of Teilhard, especially if the childish error of identifying ego-consciousness with the Logos and Light of the unconscious God archetype or *imago Dei* (God image) is avoided and the transcendent as well as numinous qualities of Teilhard's cosmic Christ are maintained. The incarnation of God ceases to be interpreted as a singular historic event. It becomes an evolutionary process through which God, though greater than the world, becomes conscious and is fulfilled through humanity as Jung also noted in passages about the continuing incarnation of God through humanity.

However, in the 1950s and during the reign of Pope Pius XII questioning Genesis, as Teilhard did, was still regarded as dangerous and the quiet acceptance of evolution as more than just a theory was still some decades away. If the Second Vatican Council can be regarded as a brief renaissance during which the ecclesiastical windows were thrown open to new ideas, including those of empirical science,

Catholic theology has not only remained static ever since, it seems to have regressed into patriarchal absolutism. God is still clad in parental garments, and humanity is correspondingly held in a state of infantile dependency and compliance through the power of ecclesiastical authority, a position congenial neither to ecumenism nor to interfaith dialogue. Ecclesiastical authority in this state seems determined to cling to power at the expense of truth and at the cost of fulfilling the awesome vision implicit in the notion of a continuing incarnation and the role of humanity as creating nature rather than passively adapting to it.

Hence, the idea of God becoming both conscious and complete through an evolving humankind is still most likely to be perceived as heretical and the notion of the divinization of humanity as bordering on blasphemy. It is almost as though conservative Catholicism seeks a return to the medieval period, keeping God in heaven, while resisting scientific enlightenment, which might guarantee a place for its rich treasure of archetypal rituals and symbols of transformation in the future of cultural evolution. Tragically, such a posture can only perpetuate the schism between science and religion while giving zealous skeptics like Dawkins good reason to ridicule theology as well as the numinous, Jungian God archetype. Dawkins is scathing in his criticism of Jung as a theist who "also believed that particular books on his shelf spontaneously exploded with a loud bang" (2006, 50–51).

I have directed these remarks to Catholicism because I perceive much that is of archetypal, universal, and timeless value in its mysticism and because its theology is incarnational, although it could be transformed and vivified by being integrated with scientific insights. Evangelical and fundamentalist Christianity, on the other hand, seems to me to be a lost cause and destined for eventual extinction in spite of recent revivals in many parts of the world. The same destiny of cultural extinction probably awaits fundamentalist versions of the other Abrahamic faiths—Islam and Judaism.

Perhaps there is a lesson for Western Christianity in the Dalai Lama's maxim that wherever a conflict exists between religious belief and scientific truth, it is science that should be accepted. In an article titled, "Our Faith in Science," the Dalai Lama wrote, "If science proves some belief of Buddhism wrong, then Buddhism will have to change. In my view, science and Buddhism share a search for truth and for understanding reality. By learning from science about aspects of reality where its understanding may be more advanced, I believe that

Buddhism enriches its own world view" (2005, n.p.). The extraordinary wisdom in this principle is that on the spiritual quest for the *logos* of understanding, it is the epiphany of truth, mathematical or empirical, that is paradoxically the most enduring source of rapturous connection to the numinous.

How could it be otherwise when the laws of the universe, as well as those of life and mind are decoded in their majesty, elegance, and beauty? Humankind will complete God not by defending ancient superstitions but by a courageous and relentless pursuit of the truth about both the internal and external cosmos. As Pauli put it, the archetypes as timeless cosmic ordering and regulating principles are discernable through their verifiable influence in both the phenomenal and internal worlds. At the risk of some anthropomorphism, I would conclude by suggesting that perhaps God needs humanity to become fully and reflectively conscious and to become an active participant in the future evolution of Mind and of the earth itself.

Archbishop of Canterbury Rowan Williams captured an insight most essential for a twenty-first-century theology when he was reported in *Ekklesia* (October 16, 2007) to have commented that "religion conceives of God as eternal and unconditioned, rather than being a hypothesis in competition with scientific ones." The scientific hypotheses to which Williams refers are like those argued by Dawkins, who speculated that a principle equivalent to natural selection might be the "explanation" of the existence of a universe (one of many) capable of sustaining sentient life. The vacuousness of this notion as a scientific hypothesis, which involves backward extrapolation of the principle of natural selection to cosmology, is astonishing and involves a species of reasoning that explains practically nothing at all about the emergence and role of consciousness or cultural evolution!

A scientifically illuminated incarnational theology can now be construed to mean the further evolution of God through humanity, as I have argued earlier in this book. It may therefore also mean recognition that the metaphysical attributes of God had become "converted to the supernaturalness of humanity," as Jungian analyst Michael Fordham suggested (1985, 179). Jung himself rejected the simplistic reduction of religion to psychology while adopting the position described by Fordham that the study of humanity must "reveal the nature of God as far as it can be understood by human beings" (ibid., 184). Conversely, humanity becomes more and more Godlike through an enhancement of awareness of itself in the cosmos and, again, reflecting its *logos*.

The Future Evolution of God

Traditional incarnational theology has remained confined by a static image of God and an outmoded cosmology. It has been frozen by the arrow of time and by a strange notion whereby a transcendent and eternal God engages humankind through an almost random series of interventions in history, most notably perhaps by becoming human in the historic figure of Christ. The myth, still interpreted by many Christians as history, is that the primordial Adam and original Son of God brought such chaos and disorder to creation after the fall from grace depicted in Genesis that the Old Testament God Jahweh was forced to intervene personally by becoming human and dying a sacrificial death through Christ to appease God and to redeem the world.

In this grotesque theological confusion of archetypal myth with history, God is dysfunctional and unconscious of God's shadow qualities, as Jung has pointed out. Humanity seems to be suffering from some form of collective attention deficit hyperactivity disorder and destined to self-destruct unless God intervenes to restore sanity and order. Fortunately, a third-millennium theology illuminated by science does not need to remain in such a state of confusion and objective disorder. Nor should such a theology be conflated with outmoded fundamentalist concepts which deserve to be ridiculed and dismissed as irrational and dangerous as skeptics like Dawkins assert. However, this outmoded form of religion has been dead for so long that it is barely recognizable in the twenty-first century, as Archbishop Rowan Williams has noted.

On the contrary, an evolved third-millennium theology could reflect the negentropic movement in matter toward ever-increasing states of complexity, order, and central organization, culminating in the emergence of reflective consciousness itself. This is made possible by Schrödinger's contraption, known as the human brain, which currently stands at the summit of biological evolution while being, at the same time, the organ necessary for the future evolution of God. This will mean completing the story of Mind and Time while resisting the seductive simplicity of identifying mind with the material processes at work in the brain. Such a sublime consummation also implies the development of an incarnational theology in which the numinous is implicit in cosmic evolution, while being completed by humankind.

The numinous principle is not remote from and intervening in cosmology and evolution, with such apparent miracles and magic as those previously invoked to account for the animation of matter and the appearance of reflective consciousness. A universe which evolves its own reflecting mirror in humanity, a mirror capable of questioning and understanding its own origins while deciding its future direction, requires no proofs by contingency of the existence of God. Such a universe, as Shalom (1989, 485) concludes in his treatment of identity and his timelessness-permanence pole of the Self, is not possible without a God. The primordial reality, which is also the eternal now or timelessness associated with the archetypes as cosmic ordering and regulating principles, is discovered in mathematical truths and empirical laws alike. This timeless reality nevertheless sustains the arrow of time while becoming explicit in both mind and matter. Completing the story of time and mind is a notion so magnificent and of such radiant beauty that I cannot refrain from referring to it as the "hymn of the universe," a label inspired by a text written by Teilhard de Chardin.

The Hymn of the Universe

This hymn celebrates the radiant wisdom expressed in the form discernible in the process of cosmic evolution which has given birth to humankind, a species in which the incarnation of God is characterized by conscious and intentional participation or active "partaking," to use Bohm's term, in the future of evolution, at the level of Teilhard's noosphere or collective consciousness. A cosmic evolutionary process, which has an implicit numinous dimension in the form of archetypes as timeless ordering and regulating principles, evolves a reflectively conscious human species through which the continuing incarnation of God becomes conscious and consummated, while manifesting a Mind and order, transcending that of humanity collectively yet revealed in such forms as timeless mathematical truths encoded in empirical laws. Such participation in future evolution will be absolutely contingent upon a global sense of identification with the species as a whole, an indispensable condition for the containment of global warming, which will otherwise, in time, render the earth uninhabitable for future generations.

Similarly, overcoming the challenge of microorganisms such as HIV and tuberculosis, which already threaten the survival of so many, will entail the recognition of a figurative quantum entanglement between the developed and developing worlds, implying a geopolitical holism which will transcend the confines of nationalism and economic self-interest. This is nothing less than a holistic vision, itself mystical, of the interconnectedness of all beings in an ecosystem that embraces all forms of life. Such a spiritual awakening will mean a transformation whereby lost unity and innocence are restored collectively so that none are excommunicated and all are included in the necessary forms of communion created by both science and religion as concelebrants vested in concern for the conservation of the earth. It is to the achievement of such unanimity and holism that religion, despite the ridicule of skeptics, has so much to offer, these being the fruits of ecumenism in Christianity and interfaith dialogue, restoring to a secular world, which has placed its faith in materialism, a consciousness of the sacredness of all people and of the earth itself.

Such an attitude might well generate the reverence for the cathedral of the earth which seems to be essential to its future survival. The sacred structure and numinous significance of this metaphorical cathedral transcends the nation states that comprise its metaphorical stones. This means that sharing in the resources of the earth needs to be viewed as an inalienable human right, so that the greed of the few at the expense of the many is no longer morally acceptable. And just as the incarnation of God is both in and for all, so also, potentially, all could participate in an extended metaphorical Eucharistic feast in which humankind as a whole is nourished, while the true destiny of the human species is revealed on a veritable mountain of transfiguration in consciousness.

For example, if the moon, which became the destination of a pilgrimage of understanding during the 1960s, comes to be seen as an energy resource for humanity, as some scientists predict, then according to a holistic vision, no national flags would be needed there. The only flag that might fly on the moon would be one expressing the restored innocence and wholeness of the archetypal, primordial Adam as a symbolic representation of humanity, participating in creation.

Michelangelo's fresco might well suggest this interpretation to twenty-first-century eyes.

Such a completion of the story of time and mind might well be conducive to mystical rapture. The details, however, need to be filled in. Returning to the origins of life may reveal much that is of relevance to the future of humanity, as the story of evolution, including the understanding of genetics and probably the quantum code, manifest in mutation, has already demonstrated. However, such linear rationality may ultimately leave the very mystery, which is the object of the spiritual quest for meaning, an unsolved riddle more awesome than the one that challenged cryptographers such as mathematician Alan Turing due to the enigma machine during the Second World War.

The arrow of time and the inevitable death of the solar system seem to imply the ending of mind as well, according to the principle of entropy. To the religion of materialism this is simply the end of the story, which humanity will have to be mature and stoical enough to accept with resignation. How ironic that this materialist doctrine should provide a picture of the end of time and heat death so reminiscent of the metaphors of eternal damnation once painted by medieval theologians. However, is this the only fate and destination that is ponderable, given the scientific enlightenment of the last four hundred years?

In the era of mechanistic classical physics and prior to the emergence of quantum theory and depth psychology, the answer to this question would almost certainly have been in the affirmative. Besides, positivist philosophy would have ruled out questions about life after death or self-continuity from permissible discourse as pseudo-problems not to be raised in polite scientific circles. An apparently insuperable difficulty is created, as I have intimated previously, by the apparent strangulation of thought by the so-called spatiotemporal hold.

As Schrödinger himself wryly put it, in his reflections on mind and matter, the arrow of time does seem to mortally wound any hope of a future beyond either one's own individual death or that of the universe, at least to those for whom the mental constructs of space and time are accepted uncritically as articles of materialist faith. So also does the reductionist materialist position on mind, which has been so seriously questioned in this book. The hymn of the universe, however, does not necessarily have to become a requiem to mourn the ending of the story of either time or mind.

The concluding verses can be stated as follows. First, if mind and matter are complementary manifestations of a primordial reality which is timeless, eternal, and not spatiotemporally bound, then the arrow of time is not necessarily fatal for mind or self-continuity. The eternal is present in a perennial now, that of an unconscious Mind, which intersects that of individual and collective humanity, yet transcends their finiteness, being coextensive with the cosmos itself. I have referred to the discovery of the eternal truths of mathematics and empirical laws which express such epiphanies, as well as the experiences of the mystics of West and East, as examples.

Second, the abandonment of metaphysical materialism as a doctrine of nature means rejecting the seductive simplicity of reducing mind to matter, including the neurophysiological substrates or correlates of mental experiences in the brain. Sophisticated brain imaging techniques such as fMRI do not solve the psychophysical problem or change the fact that neither consciousness nor phenomenological content can be found by digging into the brain, issues I have explored at length. Thus, as I have argued in discussing Schrödinger's contribution, the mind that constructed the arrow of time is not necessarily destroyed by its own creation.

Finally, liberation from the arrow of time and from materialism implies freedom to embrace a numinous dimension of being as well as self-continuity or immortality and to dispel the delusions about God that captivate the minds of materialist zealots like Dawkins. By analogy, the notion that the sun revolves around the earth remains a delusion, no matter how compelling the evidence of simple observation through the senses seems to be, and given the Copernican theory to the contrary, was itself a construct of mind once dangerous to theologians. Now perhaps, the hymn of the universe can be a triumphant *Te Deum*.

The Triumph of Freedom over Determinism

The hymn of the universe requires one indispensable condition for its composition and completion: triumphing over the apparent bondage of the causal determinism of classical science. It is not necessary for the higher purpose of establishing a case for human freedom at the level of reflective consciousness to appeal to the court of a science in which statistical causality and indeterminacy have become the jury. Freedom cannot exist either in an indeterminate, chaotic, or random world or in one ruled by the absolute determinism of mechanistic Newtonian physics and neo-Darwinism in biology.

It is not necessary to abandon the scientific concept of (statistical) causality because the real antithesis of freedom for human beings is not causality but rather compulsion or coercion of the type imposed by totalitarian states. The Jesuit psychoanalyst William Meissner, in his book *Psychoanalysis and Religious Experience* (1984), described the human potential for overcoming constraints imposed either by societal conditions or personal history in terms of the freedom that strict materialistic determinists deny as illusory.

According to Meissner it is by virtue of freedom that human beings are able to make themselves the objects of their own reflection, through abstraction and distancing from the immediate situation. Reflection introduces both time and thought to what would otherwise be mere reaction to internal or external states. Conversely, as Pribram has pithily put it, "the more reflex the reflex, the less does mind accompany it" (2004, 21). Reflection in conscious thought, whether upon the contents of the unconscious mind as they become manifest to consciousness in dreams, fantasies, and mathematical, scientific, or artistic insights or upon information from the external world, creates the condition for responsibility and insightful action. Meissner writes, "this form of transcendence, the capacity to rise above oneself and one's environment, distinguishes humans from all other creatures" (1984, 226).

Authentic freedom is correlated with self-autonomy and a sense of responsibility. To acquire these qualities is to be grounded in a sense of inner reality and cohesive identity and "to be responsible is to assert one's sense of vitality and mastery" (Meissner 1984, 239). Thus, the transformative aim of analytically oriented psychotherapy is to achieve the same goal as the great mystical traditions of East and West, specifically, the restoration of connection to the deeper Self and numinous God archetype which in turn overcomes the narcissistic predicament by facilitating its opposite state. This transformation is essentially the *unio mystica* or oceanic union with humanity and a world in need of redemption from damage to its ecology inflicted by humankind collectively in the name of the religion of consumerist materialism.

The triumph of freedom over determinism, however, transcends the predicament confronting particular individuals. The pen is indeed mightier than the sword and the beginning of all experience is the reflective consciousness or mind which has created not only such scientific constructs as those of space and time, but also those human movements that have resulted in the overthrow of tyranny in the form of such regimes as apartheid in South Africa, Hitler's Third Reich, and other totalitarian systems of thought. Without mind, neither science nor religion, nor cultural evolution expressed in liberation movements, would exist, and the universe would have no mirror in which to reflect upon itself. Such a barren universe, however, is paradoxically conceivable only to a species endowed with the capacity for reflective consciousness and the freedom to think!

Although mystics have tended to be suspect in post-Enlightenment societies, in which religion has been made a matter to be kept quiet and private, many scientists seem to have freely indulged such "eccentric" tendencies, in spite of the intellectual disciplines imposed upon them by adherence to the scientific method. This has been noted by Australian physicist Paul Davies in his book *The Mind of God* (1992), though Davies himself denied ever having had such an experience. Some of the more eminent figures include Pauli, Bohm, Schrödinger, and, according to Davies, Richard Feynman. My own reading of Penrose's accounts of beautiful solutions and a world of eternal mathematical truths would suggest that he also may have such tendencies.

I shall conclude this section on the freedom of the human spirit by referring to a passage attributed to Einstein, who in such comments as "God does not play dice" displayed his skepticism that randomness and chaos characterize the universe from which life and consciousness emerge. In his essay "The World as I See It," Einstein wrote:

> The most beautiful experience we can have is the mysterious. It is the fundamental emotion that stands at the cradle of true art and true science. Whoever does not know it and can no longer marvel, is as good as dead and his eyes are dimmed. It was the experience of mystery—even mixed with fear—that engendered religion. A knowledge of the existence of something we cannot penetrate, our perceptions of the profoundest reason and the most radiant beauty, which only in their most primitive forms are accessible to our minds: it is this knowledge and this emotion that constitute true religiosity. In this sense and only in this sense, I am a deeply religious man.... I am satisfied with the mystery of life's eternity

and with a knowledge, a sense of the marvelous structure of
existence—as well as the humble attempt to understand even a
tiny portion of the Reason that manifests itself in nature. (1931,
193–194)

In this sublime passage, it becomes incandescently clear that Einstein
had the highest regard for mystical, transcendent, and hence numinous
experience. Indeed, he was capable of experiencing cosmic religious
feeling personally. He is thus not guilty—as charged, for instance,
by Dawkins (2006, 15–19)—of that form of atheism that rejects
everything of a mystical nature while usually being converted to the
religion of metaphysical materialism. Rejection of primitive animistic
and anthropomorphic images of God like Yahweh in the Old
Testament is another matter.

Einstein's intuition seems to have been that both science and religion
have a common ontological root, one which is not spatiotemporally
bound. Perhaps, as I have discussed, this can be construed as Bohm's
implicate order, the primordial, timeless archetypal cosmic ordering
and regulating principles proposed by Pauli and Jung, or Pribram's
holoflux transcending spacetime. The person who receives mystical
enlightenment into the nature of things encodes such experiences in
the form of either science or religion, which can in turn be construed
as standing in a relationship of complementarity to one another rather
than a relationship of mutual opposition and hostility as skeptics
continue to argue in their one-sided devotion to materialism and
chance.

The vast part of the psyche that is not in space and time, yet revealed
or manifest to it in consciousness, is eternal and cannot therefore be
annihilated either by an illusion or by what mind has itself created as
a representation. This conclusion is, paradoxically perhaps, "religious"
while being also scientific, as Schrödinger saw with such clarity.

That the complementarity between science and religion, like that
between mind and matter, also expresses the Jungian archetype of the
coniunctio oppositorum (union of opposites), and restored wholeness may
be a matter of synchronicity or meaningful acausal connection rather
than one of mere chance or randomness. The search for and discovery
of meaning is itself a liberation from the bondage of determinism.
Without psyche there would be no theory to explain the outlines
and patterns discovered by science. Philosopher and linguist Thomas

Kuhn defined *anomaly* as a phenomenon or problem not susceptible to explanation within a scientific paradigm and therefore creating the conditions for a scientific revolution (1996, 90–91). The existence of mind and consciousness, crucial to cultural and human evolution, was to constitute such an anomaly for Darwin's theory of evolution through natural selection, published as *On the Origin of Species* (1859). The anomaly of mind troubled Wallace because in his view natural selection was not a sufficient explanation for such cultural achievements as speech, composing symphonies, higher mathematics, or even the theory of evolution itself, as Richard Milner notes in *The Encyclopedia of Evolution: Humanity's Search for Its Origins* (1990). According to Milner, "since he thought that the human brain is everywhere an instrument... developed in advance of the needs of its possessor, Wallace postulated a spiritual dimension in human evolution" (1990, 457). Because Wallace believed that "human intellectual and moral faculties can only find adequate cause in the unseen universe of spirit," Darwin wrote to Wallace, "I differ grievously from you; I can see no necessity for calling in an additional and proximate cause in regard to man... I hope you have not murdered too completely your own and my child" (Milner 1990, 457). The phenomenon of the human mind and reflective consciousness can now be viewed differently and not as the danger to science or to the theory of evolution, which Darwin feared perhaps due to his own classical mechanistic view of science held prior to the emergence of quantum physics and depth psychology in the early twentieth century. However, as I have already argued in commenting upon the contributions of Huxley and Dobzhansky, in and through humanity, mind and consciousness can direct the future of cultural evolution while ensuring the conservation of the biosphere.

The lure of materialism has led humankind into an exploitation of the resources of the earth and is contingent upon the reduction of mind to mere brain processes while being totally spatiotemporally defined and bound. The extinction of mind with the death of the individual and, collectively, with the entropic winding down of the universe is an article of faith in this creed. However, perhaps with the illumination into the timeless or eternal nature of mind that I have been pointing to this gloomy outlook will be revealed for the illusion that it truly seems to be. If so, our immortality may consist of more than genetic continuity through reproduction or an individual's legacy to the world of culture, whether of science or religion.

The Problem of Evil and Suffering

The problem of evil and the suffering caused by natural disasters constitute objections only to those traditional theisms in which the God representation (image) is both personal or anthropomorphic and good. Dawkins has expressed the belief that the existence of evil "keeps theologians awake at night," while making it clear that to him this constitutes an argument only against a benign or good God, not a refutation of the so-called God hypothesis (2006, 107). To Dawkins and other like-minded skeptics, traditional theology has been compelled to invent two alternative explanations or stories in order to keep God good and the presence of evil separate from the deity. Either the presence of evil and suffering has been defined as a necessary condition for the exercise of free will and intentionality in an orderly, lawful cosmos, or, in an extraordinary exercise of active theological imagination, God has been split into two beings—one of light, creativity, and goodness; the other, God's adversary Satan, a being of darkness, evil, destructiveness, and chaos. Thus traditional theology depicts an epic battle between God and God's shadow or opposite metaphysical or supernatural side for the loyalty and "souls" of human beings in the created order of the world. In depth psychological terms, however, this would suggest that God, thus constructed, suffers from borderline personality disorder, denying and splitting off God's own less than reputable attributes which are then projected onto Satan and introjected into the world as an axis of evil.

Jung was mindful of this metaphysical duality in Christian theology. In "Answer to Job" (1952a), he wrote of the "dark side of God," which was expressed in Yahweh's attributes of jealousy, rage, and destructiveness toward God's people in the Old Testament and cruelty toward God's faithful servant Job. In the myth, God subjected Job to perhaps the most persecutory treatment and sadistic torment by Satan in the entire mythology encoded in the Old Testament. In any case, humanity, represented in the figure of Job, seems, as Jung noted, to be morally superior to God, whose need to evolve would be expressed, theologically, in the doctrine of the incarnation of God in Christ.

According to this theological doctrine, if God was becoming fully human, then, as a corollary, humanity was becoming divine, an implication suppressed in traditional theology, perhaps because such transcendence kept the Light of God at a safe distance from the darkness and evil revealed in the Old Testament. To Jung, however, Christ as a symbol embodied the archetype of the *coniunctio* or reconciliation of opposites, including those of good and evil depicted in artistic representations of the crucifixion.

In "Transformation Symbolism in the Mass" (1954), Jung referred to Christ as a "symbol of the Self," indistinguishable phenomenologically from the God image of theology and, again, a manifestation of the archetype of wholeness. Jung, however, rejected the simplistic reduction of such archetypal symbols to the status of being merely psychic, regarding them as part of an objective order in the cosmos in which humanity participates. Thus, from a depth psychological perspective, the evolution of God was also that of humankind in the direction of enhanced self-awareness and reflective consciousness. The ancient, doctrinal attribution of good to God and evil to Satan and/ or humanity simply perpetuates a chronic immaturity and splitting of the God image, eclipsing numinosity from humankind's awareness of itself, while leaving the theological problem unresolved.

The problem of evil, which seems to have been such a nightmare for theology, can only be resolved, I believe, within an evolutionary framework in which mind remains neither an anomaly nor a mere epiphenomenal by-product of brain processes, as it remains for materialists. Rather, mind needs to be grasped fully as an emergent quality whereby reflective consciousness is causally efficacious in its own right, as it must be if humankind is indeed the mirror in which the universe reflects upon itself, directing science and the future of evolution alike. The same mirror reflects archetypal expressions of the unconscious region of the psyche and, simultaneously, the order and lawfulness of the external cosmos.

It is quite meaningless, I believe, to consider evil and suffering in the absence of mind, in the absence of a reflectively conscious subject open to experiencing both the external universe and the phenomenology of the internal cosmos alike. Disasters such as earthquakes and pandemics and predicted future phenomena such as global warming become imbued with meaning and value only for a world in which consciousness has emerged. The destructiveness sometimes attributed in an animistic fashion to natural catastrophic phenomena is a product of the perception and understanding of the human observer to whose ego consciousness they are manifest, the same consciousness that has formulated the concepts of entropy and negentropy.

Thus the elimination of the dinosaurs by some cataclysmic event an estimated seventy million years ago might be construed fancifully as an act of God, infuriated with such stupid creatures, or simply as a natural extinction devoid of any significance in terms of good and evil. This possibility is a totally different matter for human beings who, on the basis of reflection in conscious thought, are capable of breaking free of the bondage of strict determinism and of making moral or ethical choices. The Lutheran theologian Dietrich Bonhoeffer, for instance, chose to become a voice for the voiceless Jewish people in Nazi Germany, while Raymund Kolbe (canonized as Saint Maximilian Maria Kolbe in 1982) willingly bargained with the guards and went to his death to spare the father of a young family in Auschwitz. But there were also holocaust deniers and perpetrators of evil. Now human beings, collectively as well as individually, need to reflect upon and make choices relevant to the future of all life on earth. In this meaningful connection, humanity is not beyond good and evil. As a species, we can partake of the numinous by creating science and culture as well as religion or, through our consumerism, paralysis of will, and inaction, become responsible for the legacy of an uninhabitable world.

The greatest challenge for a theology of the third millennium may be not only the metaphysical materialism that menaces the future of the earth but also an evolving God and the need for a theology illuminated by science in which the incarnation of God is completed in such a way that the reality of the numinous is perceived as intrinsic to the human condition. Such enlightenment would be compatible perhaps with that of Tibetan Buddhism and the Dalai Lama so that apparent conflicts between scientific and religious truths are resolved in favor of science. In and through humanity, matter has been transformed and spiritualized, creating the conditions for our full awakening to the transcendent reality of God as the Light and greatness of which we as a species are capable.

Humankind is conscious of and has participated in the evil, which, as Jung noted in commenting on Hitler's Third Reich and Stalinist Russia (1961, 360), has marked our history to date in wars and genocides and now in the potential to destroy the planet which gave our species life expressing the collective shadow implicit in the religion of metaphysical materialism. This transformation in consciousness is, I believe, the divinization of the world of which Teilhard de Chardin was an introverted and intuitive prophet. It implies a theology that integrates such concepts as those of Bohm's implicate order and such insights as those of Jung and Pauli into the relationship of complementarity of mind and matter and the metaphysical notion of the archetypes as cosmic ordering and regulating principles.

The Supernaturalness of Humanity

The evolutionary process of completing God dispels a myth, one in which God remains the remote, supernatural, interventionist deity familiar to us from the doctrine of creationism rather than representing the transcendence of which humanity is capable.

Fordham devoted a whole chapter of his book *Explorations into the Self* to the mysticism of Saint John of the Cross, including experiences referred to as the "touches of God" (1985, 193). Fordham believed that the possible discovery for humanity is nothing less than "the supernaturalness of Man." He wrote: "However, for Jung I think it would be fair to say that the mysteries of religion and the supernatural attributes of God had become converted through psychology into the supernaturalness of man.... Jung attacks those who wanted to make it seem that he was converting religion into nothing but psychology" (ibid., 179). This notion is implicit in the concept of the archetypes as cosmic ordering and regulating principles forming a bridge between mind and matter and to the role of active quantum information fulfilling this function in the work of Hiley and Pylkkänen (2005). Pauli and Jung referred to the common ontological foundation from which both mind and matter emerge in a dual aspect monist concept of reality as the *unus mundus*, which is analogous to the Bohm's implicate order. Atmanspacher has attributed to both approaches "a clearly metaphysical flavour," commenting that metaphysics in the formulations of Pauli and Jung alludes to a "reality more substantial than anything that physics and psychology would characterize as real" (2011, 3–4). Pauli and Jung came to regard the relationship between mind and matter as being one of complementarity, analogous to wave-particle duality, so that one member of the pair cannot be eliminated in favor of the other.

Harald Atmanspacher (2011) and Karl von Meyenn (2011, 11) both use the German word *unanschaulich* to characterize the reality of archetypal symbols that indicate an objective order in the cosmos of which humanity is part but which also transcends humanity. Bohm's notion of a mind extending indefinitely beyond humanity as a whole and the Jungian collective unconscious with its archetypal symbols (Pauli's U-field) imply the existence of dimensions of mind and of the Self that are not spatiotemporally bound. (Pauli's concept of the U-field regarded the unconscious as the psychological counterpart of the field in quantum physics while transcending space and time.) The supernaturalness of man that Fordham posited lies in the emergent reflective consciousness through which the numinous dimension implicit in the evolutionary process is revealed and consummates itself. The unconscious God archetype emerges into consciousness in the form of images and symbols from the timeless unconscious. Such archetypal images are dramatically expressed in religious liturgies such as the mass.

In "Transformation Symbolism in the Mass" (1954), Jung referred to the liturgical drama as a rite corresponding to the individuation process. The purpose of the liturgy is to facilitate within the figurative crucible of the church a living experience of the numinosity of the archetypes, in particular Christ as a symbol of the Self, using ritual movement, sacred music, and imaginal meditation, even the censing of the altar representing the inclusion of humankind in the incarnational mystery as well as the spiritualization of matter. From a theological perspective, William Dols has treated this understanding of religious liturgy at length in his book chapter titled "The Church as Crucible for Transformation" (1987).

In and through humanity, matter has been transformed, made conscious, and spiritualized, creating the conditions for our full awakening to the transcendent reality of God as the Light and greatness in which we as a species participate as the numinous dimension of evolution (which might well cause insomnia in militant atheists; Jung, incidentally, referred to atheism as a "stupid error" (1940, 82). This transformation in consciousness is, I believe, the divinization or resacralization of the world, of which Jung, Pauli, and Teilhard de Chardin were intuitive prophets.

POSTSCRIPT

Agnosticism and Enlightenment

In the history of ideas in the West, initiation into the philosophy and methodology of science has meant adopting a position of agnosticism in relation to questions which were dismissed as imponderable or unanswerable, especially those that had traditionally been the subject matter of theology. Since the Enlightenment and the age of reason, only issues that could be settled by observation and measurement have been admitted into the domain of empirical science. Positivism in philosophy was devoted to eliminating the residues of metaphysical and religious systems of thought from science so that questions about the existence of God, self-continuity, and immortality were defined as pseudo-problems to which answers about truth and falsity were not to be sought.

Agnosticism evolved into the rationalist position of denying the possibility of knowing anything about answers to religious questions, frequently adopted after a course in making one's ideas clear, rooted in the writings of such philosophers as Bertrand Russell (1929), his pupil Ludwig Wittgenstein (1922), and the members of the elite Vienna Circle about the criteria for identifying whether concepts were corrigible to empirical observation. To positivist philosophers, religious or metaphysical ideas were to be passed over in silence as empirically meaningless. The sheer weight of authority associated with such philosophical writings, reinforced by academics, reminded me as an undergraduate student of the power once wielded by the magisterium of the Roman Catholic Church. Personally, as an undergraduate, I found some solace in the writings of Teilhard de Chardin, who had attempted to bridge science and religion. Sometimes, the newly enlightened agnostic could be tempted to adopt an attitude of intellectual superiority and contempt toward those who still clung to "archaic" religious beliefs and superstitions, adopting an iconoclastic zealotry in ridding academia and the world of such dangerous thinking. Richard Dawkins's posture of ridicule toward religion is a contemporary example of such militant agnosticism.

Prior to the transformation of science by the quantum revolution and the pursuit of an empirical exploration of consciousness, the mind of the human observer and anything of a personal nature was detached from scientific enquiry. Thus, as I have pointed out in earlier chapters and in discussing the contribution of Erwin Schrödinger to the understanding of life and mind, no God could be found in a space and time from which everything mental and personal had been excised by definition.

In the radical behaviorial psychology of B. F. Skinner and John B. Watson, mentalistic concepts including consciousness and the notion of the unconscious were excised as pseudoscientific until these notions were rediscovered in a transformed cognitive behavior theory in which the paradigm permitted the use of such terms as *cognitive restructuring* in its therapeutic applications. Radical behaviorists, like classical physicists, prided themselves on being both rationalist and agnostic while embracing an underlying materialistic epistemology.

This position reminds me again of Pribram's remark, "the more reflex the reflex, the less does mind accompany it" (2004, 21). Radical behaviorism was intentionally and zealously "mindless," focusing only upon learned stimulus-response connections while acknowledging that the rest of the story about the causes of human behavior would be discovered in brain processes. Psychoanalysis was drummed out of academic psychology departments as a pseudoscience whose concepts were both unfalsifiable and unmeasurable, and Freud and Jung, for instance, tended to be named primarily as sources of the errors and muddled thinking which students were advised to avoid. I challenged the claim about quantizing unconscious mental processes in a paper (1978) that explored ego defense mechanisms and affects as predictors of behavior and biopsy outcome in women with symptoms of breast cancer.

More recently, cognitive behavioral therapy has adopted "mindfulness," some notion of unconscious mental processes, including those expressed in transference of childhood conflicts and emotions onto others in adult life, and even spirituality into its framework after having tried to oust depth psychology and psychoanalysis from academia for decades. Even a once militantly atheistic Albert Ellis, famous for his "rational-emotive" approach and support of cognitive behavioral therapy (CBT), had become less hostile to spirituality prior to his death, perhaps because the search for identity, meaning, and connection to a transcendent or transpersonal reality is so difficult to avoid in clients, especially those who confront mortality and self-continuity. The new CBT is an effective, evidence-based treatment for such conditions as anxiety disorders and depression while having evolved beyond the confines of classical behavior therapy in approaching clients more holistically. Agnosticism can be difficult to sustain in the face of such ultimate questions as those of mortality, the search for meaning, and transpersonal reality, which have traditionally fallen into the realm of theology.

"Enlightenment" into such human conditions as those discussed by existential psychotherapists like Viktor Frankl, holocaust survivor and author of *Man's Search for Meaning,* may imply questioning a previously dogmatic agnostic attitude, as well as challenging the religion of materialism if such threats as global warming confronting humanity are to be overcome. Global warming can be construed as a direct manifestation of the materialist heresy and of the consumerism that it underpins.

Agnosticism is not to be confused with the position of atheism. Whereas agnosticism strictly claims that it is empirically meaningless to assert an hypothesis about the existence of God, atheism goes a step further and denies that God exists at all. To the true agnostic, such a negation of God is as irrational and unscientific as would be affirmation of belief in such existence. Or, as the positivists would have put it, the predicate of existence could neither be affirmed nor denied. They might well have expressed similar reservations about the multiverse theory, which Dawkins invokes in conjunction with the anthropic principle and a backward extrapolation of Darwinian natural selection to cosmology as an alternative to the God hypothesis.

According to the positivists, it would be futile to posit a God hypothesis because it could not be shown to be either true or false through observation and measurement. By contrast perhaps, Archbishop Rowan Williams's conceptualization of God as "eternal and unconditioned," seems to provide a theological perspective that is compatible with post-classical physics as well as a depth psychology, both of which accommodate concepts of timelessness. Such concepts have acquired scientific respectability since the quantum revolution and the emergence of depth psychology early in the twentieth century. Wittgenstein's notions about observables and what could be meaningfully spoken of in empirical science were already becoming outmoded at the time of the publication of his *Tractatus* in 1922.

I have argued in this book for the proposition that a rigid agnosticism with its roots in Enlightenment thought, positivism in philosophy, and a largely unchallenged materialist epistemology of science need to be seriously questioned. There is no longer any doubt about the scientific investigation of religious experience nor of the cosmic religious feelings reported by such scientists as Einstein and others of mystical disposition, whose indoctrination in the history and philosophy of science should have been a sufficient remedy for any God delusion or mysticism. Belief in the existence of such unobservables as God, the unconscious, and the operation of Pauli's exclusion principle expressed in the organization of the elements on the periodic table alike persisted in spite of such philosophical dogmatizing. However, the future of humanity and of the earth itself would seem to me to require an enhanced sense of the numinous and sacredness of all beings and things rather than the irreverence implicit in the manifold guises of devoutly religious materialism.

Perhaps a new enlightenment will heal the three-hundred-year-old schism between science and religion. A new enlightenment would restore spirit to matter while acknowledging the interaction between mind, matter, and culture. However, this would be to acknowledge the radiant wisdom in Einstein's idea that the mystical or mysterious is the source of all true science and culture. It is difficult to find much congruence between such a vision and the arid materialism implicit in both positivist philosophy and science prior to the quantum and relativity revolutions. Einstein's vision is more congruent with both a relationship of complementarity between mind and matter and the timeless dimensions of the unconscious and the Self in depth psychology, which acknowledges the numinous dimension of being fully human and participating in the continuing incarnation to which Jung referred.

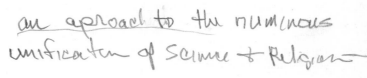

an approach to the numinous
unification of science + Religion

BIBLIOGRAPHY

Atmanspacher, H. 2007. Editorial. *Mind and Matter* 5(2):131–134.
———. 2011. Editorial. *Mind and Matter* 9(1):3–7.
Atmanspacher, H., and H. Primas. 2006. "Pauli's Ideas on Mind and Matter in the Context of Contemporary Science." *Journal of Consciousness Studies* 13(3):5–50
Blumenthal, S. 2006. *How Bush Rules: Chronicles of a Radical Regime*. Princeton, NJ: Princeton University Press.
Bohm, D. 1980. *Wholeness and the Implicate Order*. London: Routledge.
———. 2002. *The Undivided Universe*. London: Routledge.
Buber, M. 1988. *Eclipse of God: Studies in the Relation between Religion and Philosophy*. Amherst, NY: Humanities Press.
Chomsky, N. 2002. *On Nature and Language*. Cambridge, UK: Cambridge University Press.
Conrad, M. 1990. "Quantum Mechanics and Cellular Information Processing: The Self-assembly Paradigm." *Biomedica Biochimica Acta* 49(8/9):743–755.
Dalai Lama. 2005 (November 12). "Our Faith in Science." *New York Times*. Retrieved from: http://psyphz.psych.wisc.edu/web/News/NYT_dalai_lama_op_ed.html.
Darwin, C. 1859. *On the Origin of Species by Means of Natural Selection*. London: John Murray.
Davies, P. 1992. *The Mind of God: The Scientific Basis for a Rational World*. New York: Simon and Schuster.
———. 2004. "Does Quantum Mechanics Play a Non-trivial Role in Life?" *Biosystems* 78(1–3):69–79.
Dawkins, R. 2006. *The God Delusion*. London: Bantam Press.
Dobzhansky, T. 1963. *Evolution, Genetics, and Man*. New York: John Wiley & Sons, Inc.
Dols, W. 1987. "The Church as Crucible for Transformation." In *Jung's Challenge to Contemporary Religion*, edited by M. Stein and R. L. Moore, 127–145. Wilmette, IL: Chiron Publications.
Einstein, A. 1931. "The World As I See It." *Forum and Century*, 84:193–194. Retrieved from http://www.aip.org/history/einstein/essay.htm.
Feynman, R. P. 1986. "Quantum Mechanical Computers." *Foundations of Physics* 16:507–31.
Fordham, M. 1985. *Explorations into the Self*. London: Karnac Books.
Frankl, V. E. 1984. *Man's Search for Meaning: An Introduction to Logotherapy*. London: Hodder and Stoughton.
Freud, S. 1900. *The Interpretation of Dreams*. Vol. 4, *Standard Edition*. London: Hogarth.

————. 1916. *Introductory Lectures on Psycho-Analysis*. Vol. 15, *Standard Edition*. London: Hogarth.

————. 1927. *The Future of an Illusion*. Vol. 21, *Standard Edition*. London: Hogarth.

————. 1939. *Moses and Monotheism*. Vol. 23, *Standard Edition*. London: Hogarth.

Ghanekar, Kiran, Alan McBride, Odir Dellagostin, Stephen Thorne, Rachel Mooney, and Johnjoe McFadden. 1999. "Stimulation of Transposition of the *Mycobacterium tuberculosis* Insertion Sequence IS*6110* by Exposure to a Microaerobic Environment." *Molecular Microbiology* 33(5):982–993.

Griffiths, B. 1992. *A New Vision of Reality: Western Science, Eastern Mysticism, and Christian Faith*. London: Fount Paperbacks.

Hiley, B. J., and P. Pylkkänen. 2005. "Can Mind Affect Matter via Active Information?" *Mind and Matter* 3(2):7–27.

Hitchens, C. 2007. *God Is Not Great: How Religion Poisons Everything*. New York: Hatchette Book Group.

Honeywill, R. 2008. *Lamarck's Evolution: Two Centuries of Genius and Jealousy*. London: Murdoch Books.

Jacoby, M. 1991. *Individuation and Narcissism: The Psychology of the Self in Jung and Kohut*. London: Routledge.

Jung, C. G. 1933. *Modern Man in Search of a Soul*. London: Routledge, 2001.

————. 1940. "Psychology and Religion." In *CW*, vol. 11. London: Routledge and Kegan Paul, 1958.

————. 1948. "A Psychological Approach to the Dogma of the Trinity." In *CW*, vol. 11. London: Routledge and Kegan Paul, 1958.

————. 1951. *Aion. CW*, vol. 9ii. Princeton, NJ: Princeton University Press, 1959.

————. 1952a. "Answer to Job." In *CW*, vol. 11. London: Routledge and Kegan Paul, 1958.

————. 1952b. *Symbols of Transformation. CW*, vol. 5. London: Routledge and Kegan Paul, 1962.

————. 1954. "Transformation Symbolism in the Mass." In *CW*, vol. 11. London: Routledge and Kegan Paul, 1958.

————. 1961. *Memories, Dreams, Reflections*. London: Fontana Books, 1995.

Kohut, H. 1993. *The Restoration of the Self.* New York: International Universities Press.

Kuhn, T. 1996. *The Structure of Scientific Revolutions*. 3rd edition. Chicago: University of Chicago Press.

Küng, H. 2007. *The Beginning of All Things: Science and Religion*. New York: Eerdmans.

Laurikainen, K. V. 1988. *Beyond the Atom: The Philosophical Thought of Wolfgang Pauli*. Berlin: Springer-Verlag.

Matsuno, K. 2000. "Is There a Biology of Quantum Information?" *Biosystems* 55:39–46.

McFadden, Johnjoe, and Jim Al-Khalili. 1999. "A Quantum Mechanical Model of Adaptive Mutation." *Biosystems* 50(3):203–211.

Meissner, W. W. 1984. *Psychoanalysis and Religious Experience*. New Haven, CT: Yale University Press.

Milner, R. 1990. *The Encyclopedia of Evolution: Humanity's Search for Its Origins*. New York: Facts on File.

Penrose, R. 1999. *The Emperor's New Mind: Concerning Computers, Minds, and the Laws of Physics*. Oxford, UK: Oxford University Press.

———. 2004. *The Road to Reality: A Complete Guide to the Laws of the Universe*. London: Jonathan Cape.

Polkinghorne, J. 2006. *Exploring Reality: The Intertwining of Science and Religion*. New Haven, CT: Yale University Press.

Pope, Alexander. 1903. *The Complete Poetical Works*, ed. by Henry W. Boynton. Boston and New York: Houghton, Mifflin & Co. Retrieved July 9, 2012, from www.bartleby.com/203/132.html.

Popp, Fritz-Albert. 1989. "Coherent Photon Storage of Biological Systems." In *Electromagnetic Bio-Information*, edited by Fritz-Albert Popp, Ulrich Warnke, Herbert L. Konig, and Walter Peschka. Munich: Urban and Schwarzenberg.

Popper, K. R. 1972. *The Logic of Scientific Discovery*. London: Hutchinson.

Popper, K. R., and J. Eccles. 1983. *The Self and Its Brain: An Argument for Interactionism*. London: Routledge and Kegan Paul.

Pribram, K. R. 2004. "Consciousness Reassessed." *Mind and Matter* 2(1):7–35.

Primas, H. 2003. "Time-entanglement between Mind and Matter." *Mind and Matter* 1(1):81–119.

Ramachandran, V. S. 1997. "The Neural Basis of Religious Experience." Paper presented at the 27th Annual Meeting of the Society for Neuroscience, October 25–30.

Russell, B. 1929. *Our Knowledge of the External World*. New York: W. W. Norton.

Schrödinger, E. 1992. *What Is Life? With "Mind and Matter" and "Autobiographical Sketches."* Foreword by Sir Roger Penrose. Cambridge, England: Cambridge University Press.

Shalom, A. 1989. *The Body/Mind Conceptual Framework and the Problem of Personal Identity*. Amherst, NY: Prometheus Books.

Spong, J. S. 1996. *Liberating the Gospels: Reading the Bible with Jewish Eyes*. San Francisco: HarperCollins.

Steele, E. J. 1998. *Lamarck's Signature: How Retrogenes are Changing Darwin's Natural Selection Paradigm*. St. Leonards, Australia: Allen & Unwin.

———. 2009. "Lamarck and Immunity: Somatic and Germline Evolution of Antibody Genes." *Journal of the Royal Society of Western Australia* 92:427–446.

Stein, M. 1986. *Jung's Treatment of Christianity: The Psychotherapy of a Religious Tradition*. Wilmette, IL: Chiron Publications.

Teilhard de Chardin, P. 1959. *The Phenomenon of Man*. New York: Harper.

———. 1964. *The Future of Man*. London: William Collins and Sons.

Todd, P. B. 1978. "Ego-defences and Affects in Women with Breast Symptoms: A Preliminary Measurement Paradigm." *British Journal of Medical Psychology* 51:177–189.

————. 1992. *AIDS: A Pilgrimage to Healing—A Guide for Health Professionals, the Clergy, Educators and Carers*. Sydney: Millennium Books.

————. 2007. "The Neglected Holocaust." *The Griffith Review* 16 (Winter): 195–202.

————. 2008. "Unconscious Mental Factors in HIV Infection." *Mind and Matter* 6(2):193–206.

————. 2011. "The Numinous and the Archetypes as Timeless, Cosmic Ordering and Regulating Principles in Evolution." Talk given at the C. G. Jung Society of Sydney, April 9, 2011. Retrieved from: http://www. jungdownunder.com/links_main/Speakers_Presentations/Speakers_ Presentations.html.

von Meyenn, K. 2011. "Dreams and Fantasies of a Quantum Physicist." *Mind and Matter* 9(1):9–35.

"Williams Questions Dawkins' Critical Thinking about Religion." 2007 (October 16). *Ekklesia*. Retrieved from: www.ekklesia.co.uk/node/5925.

Winnicott, D. 1971. *Playing and Reality*. London: Tavistock Publications.

Wittgenstein, L. 1922. *Tractatus Logico-Philosophicus*. Foreword by Bertrand Russell. London: Kegan-Paul, Trench Trubner.

Index